'In this moving book, Andrew White, dear friend and colleague, welcomes us all into the deepest intimacy of the tears and turmoil of his life as he takes us to the heart of his relationship with God in Christ. Within his prophetic and passionate advocacy of the poor and persecuted, we find a Christian leader wrestling with doubt and difficulties, faith and failure – and finding the Lord sufficient in all circumstances.

To be truly honest, I find it amazing that, in spite of health issues that would leave most of us crushed and helpless, Andrew carries on his inspiring and international work which continues to change lives. Read this book; it may change yours!'
George Carey (Baron Carey of Clifton), 103rd Archbishop of Canterbury

'*A Year with Andrew White* is not a book of "feel good" meditations. Canon White takes us into the real world. Having spent most of his life ministering and being a peace negotiator in the Middle East (especially Baghdad and Jerusalem), he makes readers face the horrific truths of a suffering world that includes kidnapping and terrorism, a world that is almost unrecognizable to readers in the comfortable West. With each meditation throughout the year, Andrew White confronts us with the sadness and pain that are part of daily life in the Middle East. However, he insists that "the true solution to pain, destruction and death is love". This book is therefore one that will bring comfort, healing, encouragement and hope to his readers.'
David Suchet CBE

The Revd Canon Dr Andrew White currently serves as Ambassador to Jerusalem Middle East Reconciliation International (Jerusalem MERIT) and continues to speak and teach in various contexts as a respected author, lecturer and academic fellow of several leading universities, an Anglican priest and an internationally renowned global peacemaker.

As well as being the president of various organizations, Canon White is the founder of a school in Bethlehem and a primary, middle and senior school for Iraqi refugee children in Amman. His foundation also runs a community-based medical clinic and relief programme which supports Iraqi refugees who suffered persecution by ISIS and now reside in Jordan.

In addition to directing extensive relief programmes and pastoral work, Canon White continues to engage in the work of interfaith reconciliation and conflict resolution, facilitating dialogues between religious and political leaders both within the Middle East and around the globe. While his main work is currently based in Jordan and Jerusalem, Canon White also travels extensively, particularly in the UK and the USA, where he speaks, advises and lectures at various educational, academic, political and religious forums.

Also by Andrew White

Suffer the Children: Dispatches to and from the front line

Iraq: Searching for hope

The Vicar of Baghdad: Fighting for peace in the Middle East

Faith Under Fire: What the Middle East conflict has taught me about God

Father, Forgive: Reflections on peacemaking

Older Younger Brother: The tragic treatment of the Jews by the Christians

My Journey So Far

A YEAR WITH

ANDREW WHITE

weekly
52
meditations

First published in Great Britain in 2019

Society for Promoting Christian Knowledge
36 Causton Street
London SW1P 4ST
www.spck.org.uk

British Library Cataloguing-in-Publication Data
A catalogue record for this book is available from the British Library

ISBN 978–0–281–07947–6
eBook ISBN 978–0–281–07949–0

1 3 5 7 9 10 8 6 4 2

Typeset by Manila Typesetting Company
Printed in Great Britain by TJ International

eBook by Manila Typesetting Company

Produced on paper from sustainable forests

In memory of my late mentors and two closest, lifelong friends,
Lord Donald Coggan, former Archbishop of Canterbury,
and his dear wife, Lady Jean Coggan,
I dedicate this book to their daughter, Dr Ruth Coggan,
also a cherished friend

Contents

Contents

Contents

Acknowledgements

First, I thank all the members of my former Iraqi congregation, most of whom now reside in Jordan and in other nations. Their faith and stamina are a constant inspiration to me. Our memories are long-lasting and rich, full of the grace and mercy of God in times of trouble.

Second, I thank Father Khalil Jaar, who cares for so many of my people and oversees our work in Jordan. He is a faithful priest in the truest sense of the term.

I also thank my patrons, Chief Rabbi Melchior and Lord Carey, for being such a strength and encouragement to me during the time of transition and rebuilding.

A big thank you is also extended to the countless individuals and churches that have supported me, particularly Bethel Church, California; Connect Church, New Jersey; All Nations Church, North Carolina; Gateway Church, New Zealand; and Kennet Christian Centre, UK.

I also thank my beloved mother and sister, my dear wife Caroline, and my sons Josiah and Jacob for all of their love and support.

Last but not least, I am very grateful to my publisher Tony Collins and his team at SPCK, as well as Esther and Jake for their inspirational support in preparing the manuscript.

Introduction:
The agony and the ecstasy

This new book is designed to take you on a year-long journey.

It is a journey very much like the journey of our Lord Jesus, from pain and suffering to glory. I will share with you the reality of my own life, while praying that through my words God will speak to you about yours. Though my experiences have often taken place in extraordinary locations, in active war zones, I believe that, at a deeper level, most readers can identify with them.

Join me as, week by week, we journey away from darkness and despair towards light and hope.

1

I can't leave you, Lord

Where can I go from your Spirit?
Where can I flee from your presence?
(Psalm 139.7)

As I sat in the doctor's surgery, after a traumatic week, all I could
do was to think of the words of Psalm 139: 'Where can I flee from
your presence, O Lord?'

There have been times when I felt so ill I could not even pray.
I could only lie in suffering, aware of the presence of the Almighty.
Now, in the presence of this darkness, I was again aware that I was
not alone: the Lord was there with me.

For many years I have suffered from multiple sclerosis (MS). I was
diagnosed when I was 33 – a fairly average age for diagnosis. I had
just begun my new job as the director of the International Centre for
Reconciliation at Coventry Cathedral when I started to have problems with my balance and vision. I went to see the doctor and almost
immediately was admitted to hospital.

I went through exhaustive tests for about a month. During this
time my wife Caroline was in the final stages of pregnancy with
our second child. It was decided that she would give birth in the
same hospital, so we could at least be in close proximity to each
other.

I had had a lumbar puncture, to which I always react very badly.
This was to test my cerebral spinal fluid (CSF) to see if there were
any oligoclonal bands present. The presence of such bands in the
CSF is a definitive indication of MS.

The consultant neurologist came to see me: a Nigerian Muslim,
with whom I had formed a warm friendship. He told me that the

diagnosis and prognosis were not good, but he made clear that I had God on my side, so I was not without hope.

I phoned Caroline. I admit that even though I had known the diagnosis of MS was probable, I was in shock and actually burst into tears – something very unusual for me, since I rarely cry about myself! However, it was not long before I realized that Caroline was going into labour, so I pulled myself together and started to get ready for my wife to be admitted to the labour ward two floors above. When she arrived I was still feeling very unwell, but was ushered in a wheelchair to her bedside. Fortunately this birth was quick and it was not long before our second child was born. We had thought it would be a girl, but it was not! It was a substantial ten-pound boy, whom we were to call Jacob.

This certainly was a day of agony and ecstasy. It began with being told I had MS; it ended with a new son.

Caroline and the baby went home, but I was still having intra-venous steroids so I could not leave at that time. I was allowed out for part of one day the following weekend, and immediately rec-ognized how different Jacob was from our first son, Josiah. Jacob always seemed to be happy!

Amid all the activity of Jacob's birth and my diagnosis with MS, I was acutely comforted by those words of Psalm 139: 'Where can I flee from your presence, O Lord?' Little did I know that the day of his birth and my diagnosis was going to sum up the very nature of my life's work. My case may be a rather extreme example, but for many it is part of daily life. Pain, suffering and glory. As we say in Arabic: *Yom asal, yom basal* (honey days and onion days); days of sweetness and days of tears. Whatever each day brings, I am simply aware that I – that all of us – cannot go far from the Lord's presence. Whatever happens, he is there, standing close, looking at you and simply saying, 'I am loving you and caring for you.'

Even the darkness will not be dark to you;
the night will shine like the day,
for darkness is as light to you.
(Psalm 139.12)

The thousands of prayers I've received from my social media friends have made me realize that my 'family' is praying for me. Yes, they are my social media family, but they are truly my brothers and sisters, and I love them dearly.

One of my friends pointed out that, through my suffering – through the suffering of any of God's family – people are impelled to pray, and consequently are drawn into a new relationship with God. This has indeed been the story of my life. Tragedy after tragedy has taken place, yet through them people have been drawn together, praying in the midst of the crisis. Whether it is the critical health crisis of my youth, or the terrorist threats of recent years, or MS issues in the past two decades, I have been sustained by the glorious presence of the Almighty and the prayers of his people, my friends. This is my story: where can I flee from your presence, Lord?

There are times when our darkness seems so great; when it seems as if there's no hope and we say, 'Why, Lord? Why? What have I done wrong?' In our exasperation we ask very complex theological questions. How can a God of love allow such evil to happen? Our Lord's reply to us, today and every day, is, 'Look, I am here with you, holding your hand, even *carrying* you. Whatever happens, I will stay close to you, shining light into the darkness that surrounds you.'

Whatever the suffering you are experiencing, be it depression, physical pain, loneliness, separation or bereavement, to you our Lord says, 'I am here. Give me your pain, and let me gradually take it from you.'

Prayer

My Lord God, I give you my pain and my darkness; show me your light and your glory. May I be to you true sweetness and joy.

I thank you, Lord, that you are here and your Spirit is with me. Amen.

2

By the rivers of Babylon

By the rivers of Babylon, there we sat down,
yea, we wept, when we remembered Zion.
We hanged our harps upon the willows in the midst thereof.
For there they that carried us away captive required of us a song;
and they that wasted us required of us mirth, saying,
Sing us one of the songs of Zion.
How shall we sing the LORD's song in a strange land?
(Psalm 137.1–4 KJV)

To me the rivers of Babylon were not distant, strange, mythical watercourses. One, the Tigris, was just a few yards from the military cabin where I was living, in the Green Zone in Baghdad. Every morning before breakfast I would walk down to the wall in front of the river and pray. Every day the tune of the Boney M song would go through my mind. Every day I would say to myself, 'How can I "sing the Lord's song in a strange land"?' I would often feel a sense of distance, exile and nostalgia as I realized how far I was from my family and as I sought to integrate myself within a new culture and a new people. I often longed for my home church community and for the sense of fellowship, security, oneness and fraternity that the local church provides. Spiritually and emotionally, I felt as if I was suddenly in 'a strange place'. I was neither in my British home nor in my beloved Jerusalem, yet I knew that God had called me here and that he was with me. How could I sing the Lord's song in this place?

Are there not moments when we all ask this question, in one form or another? At times, we all feel as if we are in a strange land. Yet we know that there is power in praise. We may not know how to praise, but we just have to make ourselves get on with it. When we do so, we find that the Holy Spirit comes alongside us and enables us to do what we thought impossible.

There were days when I was sitting by the Tigris, trying to pray, and I would spot bodies bobbing up and down in the water. In Baghdad, then as now, if you killed somebody you just threw the body in the river. So all around were signs of death and destruction, yet in simply praising God he would come near. In the midst of praising God in the strange land, he would remind me time and time again that, like the prophet Isaiah, I had heard the voice of the Lord saying, 'Whom shall I send? And who will go for us?' And I said, 'Here am I. Send me!' (Isaiah 6.8). I knew without doubt that I was where God wanted me to be.

For all of us, wherever we are in the world, need to know that we are where God wants us to be. We know for sure that God will always give us joy in serving him, but he will also empower and enable us to do what he has called us to do.

Despite my health problems, I had always managed to do what I had been called to do. I could sense, however, that my neurological functions were diminishing considerably. In the year 2000, during one of my early trips to Iraq, I had become acquainted with the haematology doctors at the big university hospital called Saddam Medical City. In the course of my work I learned that in Baghdad there was a high incidence of paediatric leukaemia, which was believed to be caused by depleted uranium, the horrible material that covered a lot of the bombs dropped by the international forces during Operation Desert Storm in 1990.

The doctor heading the leukaemia team was Dr Abdul Majeed. I got to know him well, as I would often take groups to see him and his unit. Their dream was to establish a Baghdad bone marrow transplant unit. The team needed to go somewhere where they could learn bone marrow transplant techniques, so I arranged for them all to travel to the UK for a month of training at the Birmingham Children's Hospital. They went, learned a great deal and loved the whole process. They returned to Iraq and set up the bone marrow transplant unit in Baghdad.

Then, in 2010, ten years later, it was the same Dr Majeed who was telling me my health was deteriorating, and he needed to take action.

So many people have said they want to get me better. I asked the doctor how he knew what was needed. He said he had looked it up on the Internet! What I needed was stem cell treatment. I knew a little about stem cell treatment, but I knew that in most forms of treatment the stem cells were taken from aborted foetuses. Ethically there was no way I would allow that. Dr Majeed knew this but assured me he was going to take the stem cells from my own blood. I asked him if he had done this before; he said, 'No.' Nevertheless, he did the treatment the next day. And it *worked*! Within hours my voice had settled down, and I felt more like a normal person again.

During the treatment, the song 'Rivers of Babylon' continually rang through my mind. How could I 'sing the Lord's song in a strange land'? How? Because wherever we are, the Holy Spirit will come and enable us. What that miraculous treatment did was to make that 'strange land' the *beloved* land. No longer was it alien; I loved it now as much as I loved Israel.

God can turn your strange land, too, into your beloved land.

Prayer

Lord, you know that we too are often in a strange land. Will you make that strange land beloved? Will you show us your reason and purpose for being there? May we hear you calling us there, and may we know your pleasure and purpose.

Thank you, Lord, that you have made the strange glorious. Amen.

3

African reflections 1

The Spirit told Philip, 'Go to that chariot and stay near it.'
Then Philip ran up to the chariot and heard the man reading
Isaiah the prophet. 'Do you understand what you are reading?'
Philip asked. 'How can I,' he said, 'unless someone explains it
to me?' So he invited Philip to come up and sit with him.
(Acts 8.29-31)

As I go about my work in the Middle East and around the globe,
there have been few communities that have inspired me as much as
the Ethiopian community. The early name in Scripture for Ethiopia
is Cush, or in the New Testament, Abyssinia. Ethiopia is both
Jewish and Christian, and includes some of the oldest Jewish and
Christian communities in the world. It is not even possible to know
when Judaism started in Ethiopia. The Jewish community has traditionally been known as Beta (House of) Israel. It certainly began
in the first 600 years of the common era, by which time Christianity
was also established. There is little early written history but a very
substantive oral history.

Ethiopia is often seen as one of the earliest countries in the world
to officially become Christian. Possibly the process started with the
Ethiopian eunuch we read about in Acts 8. It may well have been
the return of this man to his country after meeting Philip which
resulted in the gospel being preached there and the good news
about Jesus first taking root.

Philip delayed his journey in response to hearing the voice
of God, and proceeded to show a stranger the way of the Lord.

This passage inspires me to always be like Philip, and to stop and show people the way of truth. I never want my schedule to be so busy that I do not hear the promptings of the Holy Spirit to reach out to those around me. Like Philip, we must be sensitive to divine leading, and willing to obey and draw alongside those who are searching for truth.

According to such records as exist, Christianity officially began in Ethiopia when two Syrian Christians, Frumentius and Aedesius, came to Aksum and started to tell people about the faith of Jesus of Nazareth. Frumentius and Aedesius told King Ezana, who ruled Aksum/Ethiopia in the early part of the fourth century, and he became a follower of Christ. From the year AD 341 he declared that Christianity was the official state religion, so arguably this was when the first, or one of the first, official Christian nations was established.

My own stories with the Ethiopians in Israel start in about 1993. On my regular visits to Jerusalem I would climb the narrow staircase that led to the Ethiopian chapel on the roof of the Holy Sepulchre church. It was by far the poorest chapel in the whole compound. I would try to speak to the wonderful priest there, Aba Gabriel. He only spoke Amharic, so there was very little real communication. I used to take him small gifts just to show him some appreciation.

Over the years I became increasingly close to him. We would just hold hands and pray in a language that we could not both understand. This was when I learned that you did not even need the same language to minister effectively; what you needed to do is be able to show true love and appreciation – and you don't need words to do that.

After many months of visiting Aba Gabriel, he presented me with a very beautiful Ethiopian processional cross. I have literally hundreds of crosses around the wall of my study, but Aba Gabriel's cross holds a very prominent place. Just the other day a friend of my son Jacob, Lidia, an Ethiopian Texan, visited her homeland and brought me back an exquisite Coptic cross which reminded me of the deep brotherly prayer times I shared with Aba Gabriel.

My other Ethiopian experience was with some of the many Israeli Jews from Ethiopia. No one knows how long there has been a Jewish community in the country. It has obviously been many hundreds of years. It was during the Aksumite kingdom that Judaism and the law of Moses were adopted in the reign of King Menelik, son of King Solomon and the Queen of Sheba, long before the rulers adopted Christianity as a main faith. The visit of the Queen of Sheba to King Solomon and the pilgrimage by a high official (eunuch) to Jerusalem shortly after the death of Christ shows that the Ethiopians had close connections with the Israelites and Jerusalem. Since then, Ethiopia has observed both Old and New Testament practices. Even though the Aksumite kingdom had accepted the arrival of the Messiah, Jesus Christ, during the reign of King Ezana in AD 341, the Ethiopian Jews, known as Falashas or Beta Israel, refused to accept Christianity and continued to practise their (Jewish) faith, which they still do today. They were concentrated in north-west Ethiopia, mainly in the northern province of Gondar and west of Tigray province. Many of them experienced terrible forms of persecution.

Falashas who kept their Jewish faith were airlifted to Israel in the 1980s and 1990s, and those who were deemed eligible were allowed to immigrate into Israel until 2008. The immigration of Falashas was halted in 2008 due to Israel's 'Law of Return', which guarantees that 'every Jew has the right to immigrate into Israel, and to be granted automatic citizenship' but does not permit non-Jews to return until they prove their Jewish roots. The members of the Falasha Mura community trace their Jewish roots to the biblical king Solomon. However, they are not eligible to immigrate into Israel under the Law of Return because their ancestors were persuaded or forced to convert to Christianity in the nineteenth century and they have been unable to prove they are Jewish. The Israeli prime minister, Bibi Netanyahu, has made clear that Israel has the moral duty to bring as many Falashas as possible back to Israel. Despite this commitment the Falashas have suffered serious discrimination and persecution in Israel. There are many in senior positions of authority in the government and the army, but the country still has a long way to go to overcome deep prejudice against them.

Many people believe that the ark of the covenant is stored in a secret location in Aksum, and a large number of Ethiopians are convinced that it still exists and rests somewhere in their land. It seems likely that the ark was brought to Ethiopia when Menelik returned to Aksum from his visit to his father, King Solomon, in Jerusalem. According to the Ethiopian Orthodox Tewahedo Church, the ark of the covenant has remained in Ethiopia ever since and is now kept in a small chapel standing at the heart of the monastic complex associated with Saint Mary of Zion (Mariam Tsion) church in Aksum. Although many believe this, nobody apart from members of the inner sanctum of the Patriarchate has ever claimed to have seen it.

The most important reality, of course, is not the location of the ark, but the presence of the Almighty among his people in this country, and the reality of his covenant with them. I pray often for Ethiopia, and believe that God will continue to spread his glory through this nation and bring healing to the land.

Prayer

Lord, we thank you for Philip, who reached out to a foreigner in his land, and for the desire of the eunuch to understand the fulfilment of a prophecy made centuries before. We ask that in both our readiness to share truth and our commitment to know you more, we will follow the example of each. We pray for your blessing over the great nation of Ethiopia and ask that your goodness and mercy will continue to spread across this land. Amen.

4

African reflections 2

TUNISIA, KENYA AND NIGERIA

The heavens proclaim his righteousness,
and all peoples see his glory.
(Psalm 97.6)

Tunisia

It is amazing how many people in the West talk about going to 'Africa' as if it were one country rather than a massive continent. In my earlier years of travelling I was just as focused on Africa as I was on the Middle East. My visits were mainly to Tunisia, Kenya, Nigeria and later South Africa. I truly love the continent of Africa and have enjoyed the time I have spent there. As I travel around the world, people are always surprised to learn that much of my early reconciliation ministry was Africa-based.

The first country I went to was Tunisia – on a trip that was more holiday than work. In our early married life Caroline and I went on several holidays there. This visit was of major interest to me because we went to the Tunisian island of Djerba (pronounced Jerba), in the Gulf of Gabès. Not only is this a stunning Mediterranean resort; it is also a place of great Jewish historical significance. As well as enjoying our breaks here, I investigated the ancient Jewish history. I had many encounters with God on the beach. The white sands became a place of respite for me, with many mornings spent swimming and praying. One day I was horse-riding and, as I rode, the presence of God was unforgettable. I sensed the Lord clarifying my call: to ministry in the Middle East and to teach on the history of the Jews.

There is a legend that Djerba was the famous island of lotus-eaters in Greek mythology. This belief could be linked to the fact that many of its people were originally from Israel and fled to Djerba after the destruction of the Jerusalem Temple in 586 BC. Much of the community is related to the original priestly Cohen caste. This has been proved recently through DNA testing.

Originally the island was called Meninx and kept this name until the third century AD. There are two major towns: Burgu and Midoun. Historically Meninx was a major producer of expensive murex dye, derived from marine snails, and according to Pliny the Elder, Djerba was second only to Tyre for the production of this valuable substance. The other major ancient town of great significance is Haribus. The island was densely populated in the Roman and Byzantine eras, and was very well known for its consumption of grain.

During the Middle Ages, Djerba was occupied by the Ibadi Muslims, who claimed it as their own – a claim disputed by the Christians of Sicily and Aragon. Remains from this period include numerous small mosques dating from as early as the twelfth century, as well as two substantial forts. The island was controlled twice by the Normans and Sicily: in 1135–58 and in 1284–1333. During the second of these periods it was organized as a feudal lordship. Subsequently, it came under the French colonial protectorate, which became the modern republic of Tunisia. An archaeological field survey of Djerba, carried out between 1995 and 2000 under the auspices of the University of Pennsylvania, the American Academy in Rome and the Tunisian Institut National du Patrimoine, revealed over 400 archaeological sites, including many Punic and Roman villas and an amphitheatre.

I continue to have a deep interest in the history of Tunisia and I have made many great friends during my time there. Whether Jewish, Christian or Muslim, all have been extremely welcoming and have had inspiring stories to tell.

Kenya

I first visited Kenya at the invitation of the Barnabas Fund, a charity with which I have been involved for many years. For some time I served on its committee, and one of our key projects was to support missions in Kenya. We were based in Nairobi, and the Kenyan Church Army headquarters were nearby, so we started working together. The Church Army was training young Kenyan men to be evangelists in the Anglican Church of Kenya (ACK). We visited Kenya several times a year and stayed for a period of two weeks each time, over about three years. During this time we had first-hand experience of radical African evangelism and saw hundreds of conversions. It was deeply moving to see so many lives transformed through encounters with the living God and to witness the great spiritual hunger.

I always enjoyed browsing the neighbourhood markets and buying wooden figures of Kenyan people. This was my first experience of supporting local medical work and visiting various medical clinics where I would deliver equipment and resources from the UK. It was encouraging to be there as a practical help and to offer significant support to the communities. I developed a strong link with the Anglican churches of Maseno South on Lake Victoria. At that point I was a priest in Balham, in south London. The Bishop of Maseno South visited my parish and stayed with us for three weeks, establishing a close partnership with the church I then served.

During our time in Kenya we spent a lot of time visiting various interreligious projects involving Christians and Muslims. I am very clear that I am not involved in interfaith activity that promotes interfaith prayer; I strongly believe in working together, but not in praying together. Prayer is about interceding and partnering with our Lord and our maker in a very intimate way. It is a private loving exchange which enables heavenly realities to be experienced on earth.

Nigeria

How good and pleasant it is
when God's people live together in unity!
(Psalm 133.1)

Soon after I arrived in Coventry, I started to develop a close relationship with the Bishop of Kaduna, Josiah Idowu-Fearon. Kaduna is in the north of Nigeria, in a predominantly Muslim part of the country. The Hausa are the biggest tribe in the area, and I spent so much time there that I started to see myself as a Hausa man.

When I first went to Kaduna there had been major riots between Muslims and Christians. It was not just Muslims attacking and killing Christians: sadly, both groups were involved in the violence. Churches and mosques were both being destroyed.

Bishop Josiah, our host, was a great Islamic expert and one of the world's key authorities on Muslim–Christian relations. There were two key individuals in his diocese working in the same field: an imam called Ashafa and a Pentecostal pastor called James. We spent time with them, looking intensely at how we could seriously work together for reconciliation. Over the months we met regularly.

During our meetings these two men became deeply inspired by the Alexandria Declaration.[1] They said they wanted the same kind of declaration for Kaduna. Over several weeks of intensive negotiations, we looked through the Alexandria Declaration. The matter was discussed in depth with the Governor of Kaduna State and with the President of Nigeria, both of whom agreed that we needed a similar document for Kaduna. After much more work, we finally created the Kaduna Declaration. The signing ceremony was arranged in the Nigerian capital, Abuja. Many people were present: religious, political, military and diplomatic leaders from around the world.

---

1 Signed by religious leaders in the Holy Land in 2002, the Declaration affirms the notion of negotiation and dialogue. See Chapter 15 for a fuller explanation.

The Kaduna Declaration became a major sign of hope to all: to the Christians, the Muslims and the tribal Hausa leaders. A monument was built in the city of Kaduna with the Declaration inscribed on it. There was so much hope that together the people of faith could be one because God is one. Pastor James and Imam Ashafa have remained good friends of mine, and have worked as significant partners in our work, even coming to Baghdad and Jerusalem. We are also uniquely honoured by being accredited as 'Peacemakers in Action', a title conferred on some of the most significant peacemakers in the world by Tanenbaum, the Center for Interreligious Understanding. Every two years all the Peacemakers come together for a major retreat.

What we learned through our work in Kaduna is that if there is no peace between religions, there can be no peace in the world. Peace does not come naturally; it requires a lot of hard ongoing work. Sadly, I could not continue my long-term work in Nigeria because my first commitment was to the Middle East. My co-director of the International Centre for Reconciliation at Coventry Cathedral, the then Canon Justin Welby (now Archbishop of Canterbury), took over the Nigeria work.

In the early days we saw 'how good and pleasant it is when God's people live together in unity'. Peace was seen, and grew, but it did not last. People stopped living together in unity, and friends returned to being enemies. Unfortunately, in the work of peacemaking there are no fairy tales where people 'live happily ever after'. Yet by God's grace peace can indeed happen, and this is what we work for and pray for.

Prayer

Lord God, how good and pleasant it is when your people live together in unity! Our prayer is that, through our peacemaking, enemies may indeed become true friends.

Lord, in your mercy, hear our prayer. Amen.

5

My friends on death row

And going a little farther, he fell on the ground and prayed that, if it were possible, the hour might pass from him. And he said, 'Abba, Father, all things are possible for you. Remove this cup from me. Yet not what I will, but what you will.'
(Mark 14.35–36 ESV)

One-quarter of my time is spent travelling the world, telling our story and raising funds. These trips are usually to the USA, Canada and the UK, but I also visit other countries such as South Africa and Hong Kong. One such trip was to Nashville, Tennessee, known as Music City because of its focus on country-and-western music. It is not just secular music: here you will find great worship leaders such as Michael W. Smith and Jeremy Camp.

I have been repeatedly drawn to this city, not because of the music, but because of Riverbend Maximum Security Institution.

One day, I met the chaplain to the prisoners on death row at Riverbend, and he invited me to come and speak to them. It was one of the most holy and profound visits I have ever made. I told them my story; they told me theirs. We worshipped together, anointed one another and broke bread together. I had never been anywhere else where I heard God tell me continually: 'These are my people.'

Strangely, these prisoners on death row reminded me of my days at the ultra-Orthodox Hasidic yeshiva in the area of Jerusalem known as Mea Shearim. Here I first learned about the Jewish concept of *emuna*, which can most easily be translated as 'forgiveness'. All these men on death row knew about forgiveness, and saw themselves as Messianic Jews. They all were believers in the God of Abraham, Isaac and Jacob, and wanted to know more about Israel and Judaism. We talked about what they needed me to bring them from Israel, and I helped them to understand basic Hebrew and Jewish practices.

I went back to see them regularly. I took them a copy of David Stern's translation of the Jewish Bible, signed by the translator himself. Before long I had got them each a mezuzah for their cell doors. I got them kippahs (skull caps) to wear on their heads. Several then asked for tallits (prayer shawls). Getting these items to the prison was fine; getting them into the cells with the prisoners was another matter!

When these men spoke about their faith, their words were almost identical to those of Lina, my adopted Iraqi daughter and administrative assistant in Baghdad. When representatives of the non-profit organization Voice of the Martyrs came to the church in Iraq, they asked her, 'How is it that everybody is so happy here when you have shells and rockets coming over all the time and everything is awful?' Lina said the most powerful words to me, and they frequently come back to my mind: 'When you have lost everything, Jesus is all you have left.'

These men had lost everything – several had been on death row for over 30 years – but to them the most important thing they had was Jesus the Jew. They all took seriously the fact that Jesus was Jewish, and because of one or two of the Christian books they already had, they knew of the dangers of replacement theology and regularly read Romans chapters 9—11. They knew that most of them were guilty of murder, and they knew that their God was a forgiving God. In one of the sessions with them, I talked about how God in Israel was just known as HaShem (the Name). This made them so excited, because in prison they were all just known by their number, but to God they were known as named individuals. Just as God was 'the Name', so each of them was a name.

They are not the only people I have known serving sentences for murder. I had one other friend who was inside for murder. He was serving a life sentence in Iraq. A former paratrooper in the British Army, he killed two of his colleagues who were working in security with him in Iraq. Like many in the military, he had gone straight into security work in the Iraqi combat zone after his time in the army. He was quite clearly suffering from post-traumatic stress disorder (PTSD), but had not received any treatment.

I was asked one day if I would go and see him, and I visited almost every week for a long time. Each week I would take a selection of Abu Afif chocolates, the most amazing product of Iraq. (The prison guards always took more than their fair share.) My friend and I would get down to serious talking. It was not long before he came to a true and living faith in Jesus. Each week we would pray together, I would anoint him, and we would share communion. In due course I baptized him. His story is told more fully in Chapter 24.

Danny's story was similar to that of the men in Riverbend: when he had lost everything, he realized that Jesus was all he had left.

I love these people totally rejected by everybody. They know that Jesus loves them, and that changes everything. In so many harsh conflict situations, the only solution has been to sing of the love of Jesus in the words of the Sunday school song, 'Jesus Loves Me':

Jesus loves me! This I know,
For the Bible tells me so;
Little ones to him belong;
They are weak, but he is strong.

Refrain:
Yes, Jesus loves me!
Yes, Jesus loves me!
Yes, Jesus loves me!
The Bible tells me so.
(Anna B. Warner, 1827–1915)

Such simple words, but with such power, telling us that we may have lost everything, but not the liberty, the power and the glory expressed so simply in the love of Jesus.

Fundamental to the whole love of Jesus is the fact that God the Father is so in love with his Son, Jesus, that he has given all power to him. John 3.35 (NKJV) says, 'The Father loves the Son, and has given all things into His hand.'

All power and ministry is in the name of the glorious Trinity; of God the Father through the Son and the Holy Spirit. This ministry that we share with the despised and rejected is a heavenly ministry. In the same way that our Lord has eternally shown me his love and care, he has called me to show that same love and care to others.

Prayer

Heavenly Father, we thank you for your great faithfulness to us. We pray that we will be messengers of your mercy, love and restoration to those whose past speaks against them. Let us be those who minister forgiveness and hope wherever we go, whether in the prisons, on the streets or in our places of work. Amen.

6

O little town of Bethlehem 1

DO NOT BE AFRAID

And there were shepherds living out in the fields near by, keeping watch over their flocks at night. An angel of the Lord appeared to them, and the glory of the Lord shone around them, and they were terrified. But the angel said to them, 'Do not be afraid. I bring you good news that will cause great joy for all the people. Today in the town of David a Saviour has been born to you; he is the Messiah, the Lord. This will be a sign to you: you will find a baby wrapped in cloths and lying in a manger.'

Suddenly a great company of the heavenly host appeared with the angel, praising God and saying, 'Glory to God in the highest heaven, and on earth peace to those on whom his favour rests.'

When the angels had left them and gone into heaven, the shepherds said to one another, 'Let's go to Bethlehem and see this thing that has happened, which the Lord has told us about.' (Luke 2.8-15)

This story starts when I was ill with my first major relapse of MS in 2002. I was an inpatient in hospital in Coventry, receiving a course of intravenous steroids, when I received a call on my mobile. President Yasser Arafat was shouting down the phone, *Abouna, Abouna* [Father], they have taken my church! I need you to come and help me get it back.'

I did not know that he had a church, but soon discovered he meant the Church of the Nativity in Bethlehem.

I told him that I was ill in hospital and I could not come yet.

A few minutes later I had a call from Israel's Chief Rabbi, Michael Melchior. He was blunt with me: 'We need you here now.' I told him I was in hospital. He said to me, 'Who do you work for: God or the Archbishop of Canterbury?'

The next call was from the Archbishop of Canterbury, George Carey, who was just about to retire. In a more civilized way, he said I really did need to get there as soon as possible. I discharged myself from hospital and caught the next flight to Israel.

When I arrived I discovered that a large group of Palestinian gunmen were holed up in the Church of the Nativity, together with many other people, and that Bethlehem was under a strict curfew, with no one allowed out on the streets while the Israeli troops were in position around the town. I was there to try to negotiate a peaceful resolution in order to protect the lives of the gunmen and also those in the church with them.

I did not really know what I was doing or what lay ahead of me. All I could do was think of the words of the angels in Bethlehem announcing the news of Christ's birth to the shepherds. They were the words of Luke 2.10: 'Do not be afraid.'

That night we negotiated about *how* we would negotiate. We spent much time with the British Consul General in Jerusalem, Geoffrey Adams. He became a very good friend and introduced us to the person he wanted us to work with: a senior member of MI6, Alastair Crooke, with whom we also became very close. Hanna Ishaq, my Middle Eastern Director, was with me all the time, and now, more than two decades later, having originally started off as my Israeli driver, he remains a key member of our team and oversees much of the work in Israel, the Palestinian territories and Jordan.

We sat in Jerusalem in endless meetings, trying to figure out how and with whom we should negotiate. Many hours were spent in travelling between President Yasser Arafat in Ramallah and the Ministry of Foreign Affairs in Jerusalem. Both the Israelis and Palestinians wanted me involved in the negotiations; I was the only person who had the trust of each side. This was the very beginning of my real role as a negotiator and a high-level reconciler. It was a deep learning experience, when the foundations of my work and ministry were laid.

In those early days I was going into Bethlehem when it was under total curfew, and there was nobody on the streets, apart from the Israeli Defence Force (IDF), Hanna and me. We would take urgent food supplies to those in Bethlehem who we knew were in great need, including those who had just had surgery or given birth.

Then the British Consul General, Geoffrey Adams, asked me for help with something entirely different. He had heard that one of the well-known Christians in Bethlehem, a Mr Nasser, had recently had open-heart surgery in Jordan. He had come back to his home on the edge of Manger Square. However, his wound had become infected and the stitches had come apart, which meant that he required urgent treatment. There was no way he could reach the hospital in Bethlehem, nor could any doctor get to him. The Consul General knew of my medical past and asked me to go and see him.[1]

Colonel Shmuley Hamburger, the Israeli army commander in charge of Bethlehem, told me the city was now under total curfew and there was no way even I could go in. I told him what an urgent situation it was – a matter of life and death. That day everything in Bethlehem was a matter of life and death, he said, and they were not going to allow me in. All I could do was pray the words of the angels: 'Glory to God in the highest and peace to his people on earth.'

I looked at Hanna and asked what on earth we could do now. We had prayed and we knew that Jesus would do something. What, I did not know. Often when you are in a real crisis point, all you can do is 'believe, only believe, all things are possible, only believe'. We could not get into Bethlehem, so we thought we would try to reach the next town, Beit Jala. We succeeded, though it was also under a total curfew. We stood in the middle of the main street and shouted for help.

Eventually somebody crept out of his house. I asked him if he could take me to Manger Square. He looked at me as if I was mad:

---

1 Before I trained for Anglican ministry, I had expected to have a career in medicine, and had qualified in anaesthetics.

he knew that nobody could go to Manger Square; but he seemed pleased that somebody was crazy enough to try. He was a Muslim called Mustafa. I had never seen him before that day and have never seen him since. I suspect he was really an angel.

We said we would pay him whatever he wanted. He agreed and took us. The streets were empty. I stopped by the hospital so I could get some swabs to take a culture sample. When we finally reached the right house, the family could not believe we had arrived.

Mr Nasser was in a very bad way. He had septicaemia and was barely conscious. His wound was seriously infected and had broken down. I had most of the medical things I needed on me: drugs, infusions, dressings and sutures. His wound was too infected to be restitched, so I knew I would have to come back. With the wound radically cleaned and debrided,[2] the patient rehydrated and given antibiotics, I was ready to leave. (The story concludes next week.)

As I mentioned earlier, I myself had been unwell at the time I was called out to mediate during the siege. However, I experienced a sudden transformation and surge of strength as soon as I arrived at the scene. I always found that, when in the midst of crisis, I felt better and stronger. This is part of God's enabling power in my work and life. Furthermore, I am aware that in my work I am reliant on the angelic hosts, who are still saying 'Do not fear.' In all truth, I do not fear, and I will talk more about this in future chapters.

Prayer

We thank you, Father, that as your word states, you are a very present help in times of need. We thank you that in times of crisis and war you are there with us in the midst of the darkness, and when we call to you, you answer. Amen.

---

2 Debriding is a medical procedure to remove dead tissue.

7

O little town of Bethlehem 2

THE ANGEL OF THE LORD WAS THERE

Glory to God in the highest heaven, and on earth peace to
those on whom his favour rests.
(Luke 2.14)

Having finished treating Mr Nasser, I was ready to leave
Bethlehem and return to our base in Jerusalem. Colonel Shmuley
Hamburger made it clear he would not be letting me depart on
my own. He instructed us to follow very closely behind him in
his white armoured vehicle - not a car, or a tank, but something
like a four-wheel drive. Everybody in Bethlehem knew this was
the Commander's vehicle and kept well away from it. I climbed
into the car with Mustafa, who was driving, and slowly we started
moving. I can never understand why in times of extreme crisis you
cannot drive at more than ten miles an hour.

As I sat in the slow-moving car, it suddenly dawned on me why
God had let me train first as an operating department practitioner,
working in a hospital operating theatre before serving in the theatre of war. God knows, long before we do, what we will have to
be doing. As I always make clear: in whatever he calls us to do, he
equips us for the duty and gives us joy in the service. That is not to
say there are not times of tears and great sadness.

We were told the main checkpoint to Bethlehem was closed,
so we would be driving to a different checkpoint. As we motored
slowly through the streets, there was a lot of terrorist activity taking
place with rockets and missiles flying around us. Suddenly Mustafa
turned off and drove very fast down a side road. Within seconds,

24

Shmuley was on the phone asking why we were no longer following. I assured him I had no idea! We finally got to the District Command Office (DCO), where Hanna was waiting for us and where Shmuley would be meeting us. I was worried about what he would say.

At the DCO, Shmuley ran over to me, gave me a huge hug and declared 'Baruk HaShem' (thanks be to God). He then explained that just after we turned off the main street, a huge rocket landed exactly where our car should have been, and it would have hit us if it had not been for Mustafa suddenly taking us another way. I really do think that Mustafa was indeed an angel sent that night to save Mr Nasser's life and mine. God does indeed send his angelic hosts, often looking like nothing we could have ever imagined, to make his kingdom known.

Fundamental to life in God's kingdom is seeing and knowing the long-term involvement of the Almighty in every aspect of our life, ministry and calling. I eventually got out of Bethlehem at midnight. It had been quite a day, but in reality it was just the beginning.

The task before us was to bring reconciliation between enemies. The next morning we continued negotiating, followed by more negotiating. The only thing both parties agreed on was that they wanted me to play a key role. It took 12 days of separate, independent preparatory meetings with Palestinian and Israeli government officials before we could establish who the other mediators and negotiators would be.

We finally reached the point where we could start the real negotiating about the siege. The key issue was where we were going to be based. It was decided that our base would be the house where the Palestinian Minister of Tourism, Mitri Abu Aita, lived with his family.

Their home almost became our home in the following weeks. We would meet all day, then at night certain members of the group would go and meet with the Israeli military negotiating team. Media people were continually standing waiting for us outside the gates, all day and all night. I remember two journalists in particular: Orla Guerin from the BBC whom I was very close to, and a fairly crazy Reuters reporter called Michael Georgy. He and I were good

25

friends, and he often called in the middle of the night if he thought something was happening that I needed to know about or tell him about. He always had one other thing to say as well: he wanted to marry Orla.

I assured him she was one of the best journalists in the world, while he was one of the worst, and there was no way she would marry him. During the war in Iraq in 2003, the following year, he found me again and came running up to me. 'I've been looking for you everywhere,' he said. 'We want you to marry us.' She had said 'Yes', and I did indeed conduct their wedding in Ireland. Moreover, at the ceremony I informed the guests, 'Today, we celebrate the marriage of one of the best journalists in the world to one of the worst.' So that was a really good thing to come out of the siege.

As the one cleric on the team, I was responsible for dealing with the various ecclesiastical issues, such as where to put dead bodies in the church. There was no real appreciation for the most sacred sites within. At one point the Palestinian gunmen turned the place celebrated as the location of Christ's birth into a morgue, keeping the dead bodies in that most holy shrine. It took several days of negotiations just to get the corpses removed.

The negotiators had obtained a list of everybody inside. It included 36 individuals who were clearly known and wanted terrorists in the eyes of the Israelis. Many of the people in the church were not known militants, but were now considered people posing great risk. The next big debate was where the people should go who *were* considered terrorists. Israel was clear that they could not stay in the Palestinian National Authority (PNA) as that would have radically increased security risks to Israel. So for several days there were negotiations about possible countries that would consider taking a few of the 36.

Wikipedia sums up the final negotiation well in its section on the Bethlehem siege:

On April 23, negotiations to end the siege began in the Peace Center. The negotiations were mediated by the Archbishop of Canterbury's representative in Bethlehem, Canon Andrew White.

The Israeli negotiator was IDF Colonel Lior Lotan, a lawyer by profession. At first, Yasser Arafat appointed Salah Tamari to head the negotiation team. Tamari rejected Israel's demands to hand over a list of the besieged militants, but then found out that Arafat had given [Abdullah] Daoud a contradicting order. Arafat also appointed another negotiation team, headed by [Muhammad] Rashid.

After two days of negotiations, the Palestinians were willing to discuss a possible deportation of the militants in the church to what a senior official called a 'friendly foreign country'. Then an exchange of fire took place. Two Palestinians were wounded, and four surrendered to the IDF. On April 30, Israeli officials said that at least thirty people would soon exit the church. Israel said it wanted to try them within Israel, or alternatively exile them. The Palestinians demanded that those men be moved to the Gaza Strip and others passed to Palestinian Authority control for trial.

The final days of negotiations were unbelievably complex. I hardly slept at all in the last few nights of the siege. I was left on a rooftop overlooking Manger Square and the one small exit to the Church of the Nativity. Who was to go abroad and who to Gaza? Eventually, on day 39, all the occupants of the church were removed by the British military, overseen by Sir Sherard Cowper-Coles, the British Ambassador to Israel. Individuals were brought out under cover so they could not be seen by the IDF. The most serious terrorists were then taken by the British military to Cyprus, where they were kept until it could be decided what overseas countries would accept them. Others went to Gaza. Our negotiations were over, but for the people heading to Cyprus there were still many days of negotiations to go before it was decided which European countries would take them.

The final events took place in the early hours of the morning. From my point of view, it looked as if it was all done. I felt totally shattered and exhausted. I could not even pray properly. All I could do was keep saying, 'Glory to God in the highest and peace to his people on earth.' The words of God, the words of life. There are times when we all feel totally emotionally drained. At such times all we can do is hold on to the fact that the Lord is here and his Spirit is with us.

Prayer

Thank you for your angels, O Lord, thank you for your angels. Help me to see your angels, help me see your glory, help me see lives radically changed. Thank you, Lord. Amen.

8
Josiah and Jacob

And like unto [Josiah] was there no king before him, that turned to the LORD with all his heart, and with all his soul, and with all his might, according to all the law of Moses; neither after him arose there any like him.
(2 Kings 23.25 KJV)

And there at the top the LORD was standing and saying [to Jacob], 'I am the LORD, the God of your father Abraham and the God of Isaac. I will give you and your descendants the land on which you now lie. Your descendants will be like the dust of the earth, and you will spread out to the west and east and north and south. All the families of the earth will be blessed through you and your offspring. Look, I am with you, and I will watch over you wherever you go, and I will bring you back to this land. For I will not leave you until I have done what I have promised you.'
(Genesis 28.13–15 BSB)

Josiah the reformer

Among the many important tasks of parenthood, naming your children stands out. For years I had thought about naming a child, even before I got married. I always wanted the name to be relevant to my life and beliefs. It was obviously something that Caroline and I discussed frequently from the time she became pregnant. What surprised me was that she had a far stronger opinion than me about what our child should be called. She decided that the name she wanted was Josiah.

I looked into the Hebrew meaning of the name and was simply overwhelmed. I loved the name in Hebrew: Yoshiyahu. In Jewish circles this was often reduced to Yoshi or Yossi. I loved the name so much. When we examined its meaning ('the Lord will save you' or 'the Lord will heal you'), we resolved to call our child Josiah if it was a boy.

The name Josiah was and remains within our family a name of great significance and purpose. Its meaning spoke to me of both my own healing and the healing of the various broken places where I sensed I was being called to minister. It also spoke to me of the very nature of Josiah's own anointed life and restorative ministry in Scripture. Appointed king at just eight years of age, Josiah was the son of King Amon and grandson of King Manasseh. Amon was assassinated when the boy was still so young. Both his father and grandfather were evil men who lived as pagans, not following the ways of the Lord of Israel.

Josiah, however, did not follow the ways of his father and grandfather. From an early age he sought to emulate the great King David. He started to restore the holy Temple, and it was while he was doing this that the lost Torah was found. By the age of 20 he was overseeing a major campaign to rid Israel of its pagan practices, returning it to the ways of the Lord. The Levites were brought back to their priestly duties in the Temple. Josiah rediscovered the law of Moses and got the masses to reconfirm their covenant with the God of Israel. He even reinstated the observation of Passover.

Josiah's reign ended early when he was just 39, when he was caught up in the Babylonian conquest. In his short life so much had been established, not least the nation's refocusing on the God of Abraham, Isaac and Jacob. He shows us all that we are never too young to start the real work of God, which means that our ministry among children should be central to our own calling. While my work and ministry have for many years revolved around world leaders, presidents and rulers, in recent years it has become increasingly youth-centred and focused on passing on to members of the next generation important messages regarding their call to be a reconciliatory voice and to serve the persecuted Church. I also help to run schools and support children. As I reflect on the life and character of Josiah, I am inspired for my service of God, and encouraged in my call to resist idolatry by seeking to put the Lord's ways first and by seeking his righteousness and kingdom. The relentless and passionate ministry of this young king has illuminated my life and ministry. I thank God for King Josiah – and for my own Josiah, who continues to inspire me with his tenacity, perseverance and insight.

Jacob the fighter

The naming of our second son was a little more complex than with Josiah. We had decided that he should be called Aaron, but soon afterwards we did not feel this name was right. By day three of his life we thought he was actually a Jacob. So Jacob he was named. Jacob in Scripture was the last of the Jewish patriarchs. His entire family remained righteous followers of God, and his 12 sons became the founders of the 12 tribes of Israel. After Jacob fought with God he was renamed Israel, the name of the promised land itself.

The story of Jacob begins with the story of his mother Rebecca's difficult pregnancy, which only came after 20 years of marriage. In the end, according to rabbinic tradition, she sought the wisdom and direction of Shem the son of Noah. He told her that she would have two boys, not one. Shem told her that both boys would be great but that eventually the older, who was Esau, would serve the younger. He was born holding Esau's heel, and was named Jacob, which means 'the one who takes the heel'. Esau grew to be a bold and fierce fighter; Jacob grew to be a man with intellectual prowess. His mother Rebecca always saw that Jacob was the one with superior ability. One of the stranger stories in the relationship between the two brothers was Esau agreeing to sell his birthright to Jacob in order to acquire food.

As you may well know, the story gets worse. Isaac, their father, was getting very old: aged 123, he was near death. Isaac called Esau and told him to go and catch wild animals and prepare a good meal for his father to eat. Afterwards, Isaac would bless Esau to fulfil Abraham's destiny.

Rebecca heard what was going on. She quickly called Jacob, and made him disguise himself as Esau and visit his father to get the blessing before Esau could. When Esau came back from the hunt, he discovered what had happened and told his father. Isaac declared that Jacob's deception was divinely inspired and nothing more could be done, though he blessed Esau in other ways. Esau was furious and decided to kill Jacob when he got a chance. Isaac and Rebecca were deeply disturbed about this and thus decided that the only thing to do was to send Jacob to Haran in Syria, in order to find a wife and safety.

Jacob departed for Haran alone. One night he rested in a field, using a stone as a pillow. He slept, and experienced one of the most memorable dreams in history.

Jacob dreamed of a ladder, from earth to heaven, with angels going up and down. As Jacob watched, God promised him three things: first, the land of Canaan would be given to Jacob's descendants; second, these descendants would be widespread, numerous and a source of blessing for the whole world; third, God would be with Jacob wherever he went, and would guard him.

In Jewish thought, the ladder represents prayer, which is our effort to connect ourselves, below, to God above. Just as a ladder has different rungs, so too prayer is made of different stages, each ascending ever higher. Whether it is in prayer or worship, the ladder does not just speak of connection with the Divine, but of a sense of 'rising' and 'ascending'.

God's promise to Abraham for his children to become God's chosen nation would be fulfilled through Jacob. When Jacob awoke, he poured oil on the stone to consecrate it. He swore to God that he would return to this place, which he named Beth El (the House of God). This spot would eventually become the Temple Mount in Jerusalem, the place where the Temple would stand, and the place of covenant and communion with God.

As I reflect on the significance of these great men, I pray that God will raise up many Josiahs and Jacobs in the generations that come. That is to say, my desire is for tenacious young men and women who are not intimidated by youthfulness, who know that their healer and their redeemer lives, who treasure the ways and the commands of God, and who have real life-changing encounters with him. I thank God for the reformers and restorers of the past, and pray for a multiplication of great men and women who will bring change, divine order and righteousness to every area of society. To have two sons who carry these names is a great blessing and inspiration to me.

Prayer

Lord God, we give you thanks that, in these great characters of Josiah and Jacob, you constantly tell us that you are a God of healing, restoration, salvation and covenant. From everlasting to everlasting, you are our God of salvation. Amen.

9

These dry, dry bones 1

CAN THESE BONES LIVE?

The hand of the LORD was on me, and he brought me out by the Spirit of the LORD and set me in the middle of a valley; it was full of bones. He led me to and fro among them, and I saw a great many bones on the floor of the valley, bones that were very dry. He asked me, 'Son of man, can these bones live?'

I said, 'Sovereign LORD, you alone know.'

Then he said to me, 'Prophesy to these bones and say to them, "Dry bones, hear the word of the LORD! This is what the Sovereign LORD says to these bones: I will make breath enter you, and you will come to life. I will attach tendons to you and make flesh come upon you and cover you with skin; I will put breath in you, and you will come to life. Then you will know that I am the LORD."'

So I prophesied as I was commanded. And as I was prophesying, there was a noise, a rattling sound, and the bones came together, bone to bone. I looked, and tendons and flesh appeared on them and skin covered them, but there was no breath in them.

Then he said to me, 'Prophesy to the breath; prophesy, son of man, and say to it, "This is what the Sovereign LORD says: come, breath, from the four winds and breathe into these slain, that they may live."' So I prophesied as he commanded me, and breath entered them; they came to life and stood up on their feet - a vast army.

Then he said to me: 'Son of man, these bones are the people of Israel. They say, "Our bones are dried up and our hope is gone; we are cut off." Therefore prophesy and say to them: "This is what the Sovereign LORD says: my people, I am going to open your graves and bring you up from them; I will bring you back to the land of Israel. Then you, my people, will know that I am the LORD, when I open your graves and bring you up from them. I will put my Spirit in you and you will live, and I will settle you in your own land. Then you will know that I the LORD have spoken, and I have done it, declares the LORD.'" (Ezekiel 37.1–14)

We too are called to bring life to dry bones. People often ask me about my methods of evangelism in Iraq. I have to be honest and say that I have never preached to my Muslim friends. I do not have any magic apologetic tools. Have I seen many come to faith? Yes, many. Have I seen many who want to be baptized? Yes, many.

When I consider the story of the 'dry bones', I want to tell you some true stories, though it is too dangerous to mention the real names of the people involved, so they have all been given other names.

The first story is about Ali. He was from the area known as al-Anbar, which is also called the Sunni Triangle. It is the region that Saddam Hussein came from. Everybody in that area was originally a member of Saddam's Baath Party. After the 2003 war, people from al-Anbar were often imprisoned by the coalition forces as part of what became known as the 'de-Baathification process'. Ali was one of them.

He was held captive by the US Marines in a makeshift prison. While there, he was acutely aware that Jesus kept coming to him and saying, 'Follow me.' He got hold of a US Army Bible and started reading the New Testament. He asked various soldiers about what he had read and some of them told him, 'Jesus is real' and 'He loves you.' Eventually the authorities realized that Ali posed no risk to the country and he was released from prison. He went into the centre of Baghdad and visited many of the different churches, telling the priests that he wanted to become a Christian. They all told him point blank that he was Muslim and could not become a

Christian. Finally he came to me at St George's Church. I welcomed him into our midst, asked him to dinner, loved him, heard his story and had him return to see me many times. It was clear that he was an example of dry bones wanting life.

I started taking Ali through the Alpha Course, the popular introduction to Christianity. At that time many Iraqis were coming to St George's, and we had over two thousand people doing the course. Ali would sometimes come in quietly and sit at the back of the main sessions I was leading in the church, but he would never talk to anybody. In my private sessions with him, I made it clear that he could not mention me to anyone, even his wife, or tell anyone that he was becoming a Christian. So he told nobody.

Before long I agreed to baptize him. I took him quietly into the church and baptized him with nobody else present at all. He without doubt became a faithful follower of Jesus. Still frightened about coming to the Iraqi church service, for several years he came to the main US Embassy services that I would lead. People knew Ali's story there, and among the embassy congregation he was totally safe.

Ali was by far from being the only one. When our church restarted after the war in 2003, there was a group of Mandaean converts. Mandaeans, or Sabians as they are also known, are first mentioned in the book of Job. They eventually became the followers of John the Baptist. They have all their services in water, and their place of worship is like a swimming pool. They were very involved in the church and had been to an Alpha Course conference in Amman, Jordan. They arrived safely at the conference, but on their way back to Baghdad, while in the Sunni triangle, they were kidnapped. They were never seen again. Eight of them were taken. For months there were stories of people who supposedly knew where they were. We soon learned that these were just stories without foundation, the type that gain currency after every kidnapping.

Another person whose 'dry bones' now live was a woman who was forcefully married to one of Saddam's senior government leaders. She was a serious committed Christian. She cried so much about what had happened. She had a young son as a result of this marriage. He was called Muhammad. After the war the husband was killed at the same time as Saddam's sons, Uday and Qusay. She approached me and begged me to baptize her son. I talked to him and he told me how much he had always loved Jesus and he wanted to follow Jesus for ever. Once again there were fears about baptizing him at the Anglican church, so I baptized him secretly in the Embassy. After the service he came up to me very excited with water running down his hair (we always used a lot) and he said, 'I feel new now.'

He then put his arms around me, smiled and said, 'Will you be my daddy now?' Of course I said 'Yes'. Ever since that day, wherever I am in the world, he phones me every week to pray for me at length.

The next person I want to talk about is Mahdi. He was from the family of one of the very senior ayatollahs. He saw me on TV several times, and his teacher at school was a relative of my closest friend, the British evangelist J.John. Mahdi arranged to come and see me in England. It was a wonderful meeting and we immediately became friends. Just a few weeks later he came to see me at the church in Baghdad. Once again it was a truly amazing encounter. When he came to our young people's meeting at church, he radically met with God and he knew he wanted to follow the Lord Jesus for ever. I knew there was no way I could ever baptize him in Iraq. If I was caught, I would be in grave danger. I therefore got my friends at Holy Trinity Brompton to baptize him, and renamed him Moses, for he had come through the waters to new life.[1] I chose this name for him and he agreed because 'Mousa' ('Moses' in Aramaic) is similar to his birth name.

There are many other stories like these of people who moved from being dead dry bones to being the vibrant living children of God. Moses saw my love for Rabbinics and Judaism and is now studying Hebrew and Judaism, and has even been to Israel with me. These dry bones now live, and God will use all these people as channels of his justice, love and peace. These are all stories of his glory of heaven come to earth. These stories concern not just men but women and children too.

---

1 See Genesis 2.1-10.

Prayer

We saw the dry bones in the valley, O Lord. At times we too feel so dry, yet we come to you and you make dry bones come alive. As you made all these people come alive, so you do with us, O Lord.

Come, Lord, and where there is death bring life. Thank you that you are indeed the God of creation and revelation. Amen.

10

These dry, dry bones 2

A PLACE OF ABUNDANT LIFE

Thus says the Lord GOD to these bones: 'Surely I will cause breath to enter into you, and you shall live. I will put sinews on you and bring flesh upon you, cover you with skin and put breath in you; and you shall live. Then you shall know that I am the LORD.'
(Ezekiel 37.5-6 NKJV)

My return to St George's, Baghdad, was divided into two very clear parts. The initial return was in 1998 when I first went to Iraq. The church was a classic example of dry, dead bones. It had been closed since 1990 due to British and American involvement in the Gulf War that year. The building was derelict, redundant, and had no signs of life. The only sign that there had ever been any life was a dead pigeon on the floor of the sanctuary. All the contents of the church had been removed apart from the font, which was too heavy to steal. Everything else had been taken – the pews, organ and even some of the stained-glass windows. The place had been ravaged.

I knew from Bishop Clive Handford, who was the Bishop of Cyprus and the Gulf at the time, that a caretaker had been installed. He lived in the run-down church hall, but it was evident to me that he was taking no care of the church whatsoever. Everything in the building spoke of death and destruction. Here was a classic example of dry bones that needed reviving.

When I was there from 1998, every Sunday I would try to hold a simple service in the church. The congregation was only ever made up of my team who had come with me from the UK. A short while later we were joined by some members of the United Nations staff, who turned out to be real friends. I will never forget the head of the UN staff at the time, Count Hans-Christof von Sponeck. He attended services with me regularly, and eventually he was awarded one of our early Coventry Cathedral peace prizes.

The major change in the church's identity happened after the war in 2003 due to Operation Iraqi Freedom. Soon after the war had taken place, I reopened the church, by which stage it was at least clean. We brought in some plastic disposable chairs, and our first service was certainly a memorable occasion.

The initial service was led by my close colleague and co-director of the International Centre for Reconciliation: now Archbishop Justin Welby. Among the congregation we had senior representatives from the British and American coalition bases and a very significant number of top diplomats, including the heads of the CIA and FBI, and senior figures in the British coalition such as Sir Jeremy Greenstock and Christopher Segar.

Even at that early stage of reconstruction, the Americans were persistent in voicing their belief in the separation of Church and State, which in Iraq meant a separation between religion and politics. Anyone who has any experience of politics or religion in the Middle East will realize that in reality religion and politics cannot be separated there. I remember having in-depth conversations with Iraqi political, military and religious leaders in the early days after the coalition victory, when they stated clearly that there was no separation between religion and politics.

After the initial celebrations following the fall of Saddam and his regime, the violence throughout Iraq commenced. It became obvious that the coalition diplomatic and military staff would no longer feel safe worshipping outside the Green Zone in Baghdad. It was at this stage that it was decided to establish a proper chaplaincy within the coalition headquarters in Saddam's old palace. Evidently St George's would no longer be a place of worship for the British and Americans, so the coalition services there were ended. Immediately after this, there was an influx of Iraqis to the church. We were faced with an incredible situation in which the church services were increasing in size by nearly a hundred people per week. It was very much a case of 'out with the old and in with the new' as revival and renewal started to take place before our eyes.

Suddenly, we were faced with a classic example of dry bones coming back to life. The 'church', which was dead (both in terms of the dilapidated building and the absence of worshippers), had been breathed into and 'resuscitated' by the Holy Spirit. Flesh, muscles and sinews were coming back to these dead dry bones. No longer was this a place of death, but rather a place of abundant life. As we know, like attracts like, and so it was that we multiplied rapidly and became a great beacon of light within one of the darkest places in the Middle East.

The relationships I formed with the people in that church bring me great joy to this day. We know that the 'body of Christ' is called to be united and relational. Of notable significance was the incredible expansion of ministry among the children. Officially, I was called 'Abouna' in the church, which would best be translated as 'Daddy'. In essence, we were not a 'congregation with a vicar', nor were we 'a flock with a shepherd or a pastor': we were a family with a father.

The children rapidly started learning basic English, and the first word they all learned was simply 'Daddy'. To them, I was their dad. Even though all of the children had their own families, many of them unofficially 'adopted' me as their spiritual and practical daddy. To this day, they still see me as their spiritual father and call me by this name. I have had the joy and honour of being part of their journey from early infancy to marriage. All of them, apart from one, now live abroad, having been granted residence elsewhere. Several of them now have their own children who call me 'Jeddu', which means 'Grandfather'. I have baptized all of them and continue to cherish the wonderful relationship I have with my honorary children and grandchildren.

When it was time for the children to get married, I once again had to take on the serious Iraqi role of being their father and approving who they would become engaged to. In 'letting go' and accepting the changes of season, we saw new life emerge. God's governance is ever increasing and the new generations will arise and take their place in the kingdom.

However hopeless a situation may seem, restoration and resurrection life always overcome death. Let us not forget that our Father is more concerned about the establishment of his Church and the communities of worshippers than we are. He is the one who builds his Church.

Prayer

Dear Lord, we thank you for your restorative and redemptive power to bring life to situations and circumstances that at so many times appear to be 'dry bones'. We thank you for your guidance and your counsel in enabling us to bring life to individuals and communities around us. We pray that you will continue to use each one of us to play a part in bringing transformation to others. Amen.

11

Cast all your care on him

Come to me, all you who are weary and burdened, and I will
give you rest. Take my yoke upon you and learn from me, for I
am gentle and humble in heart, and you will find rest for your
souls. For my yoke is easy and my burden is light.
(Matthew 11.28–30)

We often hear how our Lord's yoke upon us is easy and his burden is light, yet we ask ourselves: can this really be true when we are
faced with such terrible crises? I refer here not simply to those living
in war-torn countries, but to all of us who have and continue to face
great difficulties in our own lives, whether in Baghdad, London or
New York. Life can be so hard.

Yet, however hard our circumstances, we always know that we
are not alone, because the Lord's promise is to never leave us or
forsake us. I have learned to speak openly with God and tell him
how difficult my situation is. When I have cast my cares upon
him and laid down my burdens at his feet, I start praising and
worshipping him. Then, and only then, does the burden begin to
become light.

In my years in Iraq before and after the invasion of 2003,
people often asked me if I had ever met Saddam Hussein. I never
did, but I spent a lot of time looking at him, sitting just three
feet away from him in court. During his trial I would regularly
spend a morning in the courtroom. These were strange visits, but
also times of real encounter with the Almighty. Each time I went
through the intense security procedures to enter the court, I was
acutely aware that I was in the presence of God and carried the
presence of God.

I was also in the presence of one of the most evil men in history, and it was strange to be sitting just two or three feet behind him. We would frequently be looking directly at each other. Though we had never met, he probably had seen a lot of me on TV in the years before the invasion, when I was one of the very few non-Iraqis in the country. We would just look directly at each other for several minutes at a time. I would often pray for him. That was not easy; but I was challenged by those regular words of Jesus to love your enemies. I simply prayed, 'Lord, please make yourself known to him', and I allowed the divine reality of Christ in me and Christ with me to override every feeling of repulsion regarding the darkness that this man carried.

At the other end of the court was one person I did not know but really prayed for. That was the Chief Justice, Judge Rauf Rashid Abd al-Rahman. He had an extremely difficult, complex and high-profile judicial case to preside over. I knew that his job was not easy nor his burden light, but I prayed it would be. The reality was that he was not the first judge to sit over the trial; the others had not survived more than a few sessions. So frequently I would simply pray, 'Come, Lord Jesus. Judge Rauf needs you.'

Abd al-Rahman was the Minister of Justice of the Kurdish Regional Government of Iraq and a very prestigious judge and politician. His family had suffered during the attacks on his home town of Halabja, when poisonous gas was used. This first trial of Saddam was one of a long series that were lined up; however, as he was sentenced to death during this trial, the ensuing ones never actually took place.

It was a huge pressure on any judge to oversee this trial, but in the end Judge Rauf saw it through. He sentenced Saddam to death, and under Iraqi law this ruling had to be carried out in a certain number of days. The sentence was passed and the execution took place in Baghdad.

A few days later I was in Kurdistan and somehow Judge Rauf learned that I was there. He sent a message that he wanted to see me; he knew who I was but had never met me. I had acquired a reputation as a person who could make anything happen. Judge

Rauf wanted me to organize something of great importance for him.

It turned out he was suffering from serious cervical sclerosis in his neck. Major surgery was required and he wanted to know if I knew somebody who could do it in England. As soon as I returned to the UK, I tracked down the people who could undertake this surgery. One of the foremost specialists in this area was actually based on the south coast and lived not too far from my home. This was one of those occasions when I knew that, with the Lord, the case would be easy and the burden light. It was totally in the hands of the Lord and we made this clear to the judge: he agreed!

I met the surgeon in question with all of Mr Rauf's notes, X-rays and MRI scans. The doctor was a distinguished man, an Iranian educated in England. He confirmed that he could do the surgery. It was a major operation, and Judge Rauf would need to spend a considerable time in hospital before and after.

Mr Rauf's family would be travelling with him to the UK, and I knew that I would need a very select team – just a couple of people – to be with them and support them throughout the process. I knew that one such person would be our friend, Brian Futcher. He had a rather crazy second-hand shop that was called Squirrels, and so he was known to me as Brian the Squirrel. His passion in life just happened to be Christian ministry in Kurdistan, which he visited every year, going regularly to Mr Rauf's home region. Brian had a limited amount of time to give during the week, but agreed to do whatever he could.

I needed one other person to act as helper, driver and carer for the family. I asked the Almighty who it should be and he swiftly showed me a lady called Elaine, who at that point I hardly knew. I had first met her on a church visit to Leicester; her husband, who had suffered with serious muscular dystrophy, had recently died. For some reason, she had moved to the very town where Mr Rauf was having the surgery. She was overjoyed to be asked to help and agreed to carry out the task in full. She could be present most of the time.

Eventually, everything and everybody was in place. We organized Mr Rauf's visas and his travel to the UK with his wife and two daughters. So much to do, so many security issues to take seriously, but eventually it was all done. They arrived and it all worked out smoothly.

The day eventually came. Before Mr Rauf went down for surgery, we all met around him and prayed for him, which he really appreciated. While the surgery was happening, a group of people prayed continuously. The operation took several hours, but thankfully all went well and he was soon recovering in intensive care, so our intercessions turned into prayers of praise. Within a few days he was back in the normal ward, and we were all giving thanks to God for what had happened.

Elaine and Brian did everything for the family that they could, and they all became great friends. Eventually, Mr Rauf was discharged from hospital and the whole family went to spend a few days in a local hotel. In due course he went to London to enjoy a longer break with his family. On the way back to London they stopped off for tea at my home, and my young son Jacob was so pleased to meet the judge who, as he said, got rid of the evil Saddam. The stories in the Iraqi press were full of accounts of how the family had fled to the UK seeking asylum. Nobody knew the true story.

Soon after the Raufs returned to Erbil, both their helpers went to stay with them. Nobody really believes Elaine when she says that she cared for the judge who sentenced Saddam. I remain a great friend of the family and still spend time with them when in Erbil.

The story has a wonderful ending: when Elaine remarried, she and her fiancé asked me to perform the wedding ceremony in the garden of Christ Church, Jaffa Gate, Jerusalem. It was a day of great rejoicing. It all seemed easy and the yoke seemed light. At the time, everything had appeared so hard, but with the Almighty it was easy. He is our enabler and our burden-bearer, even at the most difficult of times.

Prayer

Thank you, Father, that even in times of great trial and darkness and injustice, you are a just judge. We pray that you would release divine righteousness and justice upon the earth and empower your people to bring healing to the nations.

We thank you that even when we face oppressive challenges, you are there to remove our burdens and to walk with us through every situation. Amen.

12

Baptismal adventures

Then Jesus came from Galilee to the Jordan to be baptised by John. But John tried to deter him, saying, 'I need to be baptised by you, and do you come to me?' Jesus replied, 'Let it be so now; it is proper for us to do this to fulfil all righteousness.' Then John consented.

As soon as Jesus was baptised, he went up out of the water. At that moment heaven was opened, and he saw the Spirit of God descending like a dove and alighting on him. And a voice from heaven said, 'This is my Son, whom I love; with him I am well pleased.'
(Matthew 3.13–17)

Baptism is at the very heart of our Christian faith, and our greatest model was Jesus himself. Baptism is all about purification, allegiance, and a 'sealing' of our hearts as we enter into the fullness of the Father, Son and Spirit. It is about leaving the past behind as we descend into the waters and enter into resurrection and the fullness of what Jesus did for us,

having been buried with him in baptism, in which you were also raised with him through your faith in the working of God, who raised him from the dead.
(Colossians 2.12)

As an Anglican priest, I have been involved in traditional child baptisms and also child dedications within other church streams. All of these are precious moments when God is publicly given ownership of lives dedicated to him. I have also participated in countless adult baptisms and, with each one, I have never lost the sense of awe and wonder at what this powerful act represents:

> This water symbolises baptism that now saves you also – not the removal of dirt from the body but the pledge of a clear conscience towards God. It saves you by the resurrection of Jesus Christ.
> (1 Peter 3.21)

It is a deep holy reality to give oneself back to one's creator and, as the apostle Peter states, make a pledge of living purely before him. We must never forget that the role of the baptizer is as important, and as sacred, as the role of a midwife.

Some of the earliest child baptisms I performed were in my London parishes during my early days as a vicar. I will always remember four in particular, as they were newborn babies who were very critically ill and the chances of them surviving were small. Not only did God save these babies, but all of them are alive now and a great blessing to those around them.

In the Middle East, baptism is taken as a very big declaration of Christian faith, both to those who are born into the faith tradition and to those who choose to follow Christ and leave their original tradition. For the latter group it can be a life-changing and life-threatening decision. To be baptized is to say, 'I am making a decision that will change my life and identity for ever.' Many literally put their lives at risk by choosing Jesus.

As I mentioned in an earlier chapter, the only object that had not been stolen from the derelict building of St George's Church when we first moved in was the font. It was here that I baptized many of our babies – children who are now at my school in Marka, Jordan, and whose faith in Jesus and Christian identity is as real as I have ever seen.

Easter 2004 was our first baptism service, and we used Saddam's former private swimming pool as a baptistery. As you can imagine, it was very clean, modern and palatial, decorated with tiles lined with gold. Suddenly the very space that had been used for the entertainment and self-indulgence of one of the most evil tyrants in history was becoming a space of divine worship, a place where God was being exalted. Not only did this add to the significance of the many baptisms that took place there, but it was also a great prophetic picture of divine reversal and the faithfulness of God. Kingdom living often involves taking territory and claiming space, and for us the taking of Saddam's pool was a deeply powerful symbol.

Several converts from Islam to Christianity were baptized in the pool as it was too dangerous for them to be baptized in the church – once again a powerful statement of allegiance, liberation and new identity in the very pool of the dictator to whom this nation had for so long been enslaved. One memorable day was when various American soldiers from the embassy chapel came to be baptized, as well as other soldiers from the coalition, from South Korea.

It was the first Easter Sunday after the end of the war. I discovered that the members of the choir, who were singing 'Because He Lives', were Wheaton College graduates. I was already teaching at Wheaton, and Billy Graham, who studied there, had been instrumental in my life in the Middle Eastern years. Now we were in Saddam's palace celebrating the resurrection of Jesus through corporate worship and individual baptisms. I thought Billy Graham would have been delighted to know that his old college was represented at this event.

When praying during the previous week on what to speak about, I had woken up on Good Friday morning singing that very song about being able to face the future with Jesus, and this is why I had asked the choir to sing it. For all of us, no matter what our situation – war, torment, persecution, trauma or illness – because Jesus lives, we can face tomorrow. If he did not live, our reality would be so terribly different.

This baptismal service put me in mind of another significant group in Iraq, the Mandaeans, who may be traced back to the original disciples of John the Baptist. At that point there were around 70,000 living in Iraq, and they had been harshly persecuted. They performed all of their baptisms in the River Tigris and, as I mentioned in an earlier chapter, their church services were literally held in water. Despite the fact that their doctrines are radically different from those of Christianity, their symbol of a cross with a towel round it always reminds me of the centrality of the death and resurrection of Jesus to baptism (see Figure 1). It is not an empty ritual: it relates to a historical and eternal reality and must not be taken lightly.

At present, most members of my remaining Iraqi congregation reside in Jordan. Several have obtained visas to Canada, the USA and Australia, while those left in Jordan live in hope that they will soon be granted a new homeland and a future for their children. Church life continues as normally as possible in Marka, Amman, and the Latin church that is part of our school building is where we now celebrate child baptisms. These are always very prayerful and emotional events.

As for the adults, many of the baptisms that I conduct now take place in the River Jordan. I enjoy conducting baptisms here even more than I do in Galilee because it is the place where Jesus himself was baptized. Tell Radragh is the modern name of Aenon near Salim, which is the location referred to in the Bible as the site where John the Baptist baptized his followers and was likely to have baptized Jesus. The name Jordan means 'descending', as it is here that

Figure 1 **The central symbol
of the Mandaeans – a cross
draped with a towel**

the Spirit descended as a dove and it is through baptism that so many descend into the death of Jesus and arise into the fullness of his resurrection. As we learn from Scripture, the River Jordan is a place of much activity – not least a place of miracles, healing and purification.

Many people have a sentimental relationship to biblical sites as if somehow they are holy and superior to other magnificent locations around the world. My own conviction is that land has a memory, and creation stores within itself the stories of the past. This is why I like to baptize in the Jordan.

As we conclude this chapter, let us all dwell on the most important of realities, which is the 'breaking off of the past' and the 'embracing of the new' that baptism represents. It is not about location; it is about revelation. And this great revelation is that in Christ all things are made new. This is at the very heart of all of my work:

> Therefore, if anyone is in Christ, the new creation has come: the old has gone, the new is here! All this is from God, who reconciled us to himself through Christ and gave us the ministry of reconciliation.
> (2 Corinthians 5.17–18)

Prayer

We thank you, heavenly Father, that in you we have new life and that in you we truly find ourselves. We thank you that to find you is to find mercy, sanctification and fullness of life. Amen.

13

Habakkuk

The Sovereign LORD is my strength;
he makes my feet like the feet of a deer,
he enables me to tread on the heights.
(Habakkuk 3.19)

As I read the Old Testament, I particularly enjoy the works of the minor prophets, especially as I have visited so many of their tombs, and so much of their message related to what is now Iraq. One of my favourite prophetic books is Habakkuk. Though it is a short book, it is an extremely rich part of Scripture and full of revelations concerning the nature of God. The name Habakkuk means 'embracing', and for me this speaks of the prophet's call to receive the word of truth and his faithfulness in embracing the oracle of the Lord and delivering this divine message to the people.

It is probable that Habakkuk was a contemporary of Jeremiah and prophesied between 638 and 608 BC, at a time of terrible political and moral crisis. Research also indicates that he may have been a Levite connected with the temple music. If this is the case I would not be surprised, as there is such a deeply worshipful and psalm-like tone to the last third of his oracle.

As Nahum had prophesied, the fall of Assyria was imminent and this was due to its oppression of Israel. Nahum had made clear that while God was indeed slow to anger and a refuge to the righteous in times of trouble, the obstinacy of his people in refusing to forsake their idols and in welcoming injustice and perversion was about to lead once again to their downfall.

Babylon was brought against Assyria to destroy it, and now in Habakkuk we see this same nation being used to come against

Judah. While Habakkuk accepts that God will judge the guilty, the Babylonians are considered even worse than either Assyria or Judah. God responds by instructing Habakkuk to write down a vision about an appointed time in which the Lord will bring judgement against Babylon. However, God does not refer simply to Babylon. We see that Habakkuk – like Nahum, Joel and the other prophets – uses cosmic language that boldly confronts the wickedness shared among all evil nations and proclaims the universal supremacy of God and the perfection of divine justice.

There are several aspects of Habakkuk that attract and inspire me. First, there is much to be learned from his prophetic attentiveness not simply to listen to hear the voice of God, but also to use his spiritual eyes to 'see' what God was saying and doing. On many occasions in Baghdad I relied on this 'seer' capacity, this reliance on my inner spiritual eyes to discern evil from good, and today I am learning more to rely on vision and to expect God to speak to me in this way. In the opening verse of Habakkuk chapter 2 we read:

> I will stand at my watch
> and station myself on the ramparts;
> I will look to see what he will say to me.

We do not always consider 'looking' to see what God will speak, or to associate his speaking to us through an inner voice with the 'sensing' and spiritual perceptions that we may experience. However, Habakkuk teaches that this same sense of knowing and hearing often demands our gaze, our eyes, our full attention. This posture that Habakkuk adopts on his ramparts speaks to us of the stillness, resoluteness and watchfulness that is required to hear God fully. It reminds us of the need to rid our minds of the clutter and debris that so often impedes our vision. This clutter may include negative emotions, ungodly motives, or even intellectual mindsets that prevent us from receiving the divine messages.

A second aspect that I cherish within Habakkuk's message is the prophet's declaration in verse 14 of the same chapter that:

the earth will be filled with the knowledge of the glory
   of the LORD
as the waters cover the sea.

Many of us know this verse well or have heard it quoted in different contexts, because it has informed the lyrics of many worship songs. Yet we must not allow ourselves to become so familiar with Scripture that we lose the sense of awe and profound elation that it embodies. It is not simply the glory, the weighty presence of God, that will fill the entire earth as every tongue confesses and bows to the Messiah; it is the *knowledge* of this. Nothing will be concealed or restricted. The kingdom will arrive in fullness. All systems of worldly knowledge and all structures of worldly fame and value will diminish in the light of the superior manifestation and recognition of his glory. The earth will not merely contain the knowledge of his glory; it will be filled. As the prophet proclaims, his majestic splendour will be like that of the rising sun, and the power that is hidden in his hands will flash forth like rays of light (Habakkuk 3.4). The earth will know that he is sovereign.

A third aspect that so deeply inspires me about the prophet's oracle appears in Habakkuk 3.17–18:

Though the fig-tree does not bud
and there are no grapes on the vines,
though the olive crop fails
and the fields produce no food,
though there are no sheep in the sheepfold
and no cattle in the stalls,
yet I will rejoice in the LORD,
I will be joyful in God my Saviour.

In many ways, this passage was our anthem during the dark years in Baghdad. It was the intentional stepping into divine joy, and the protection of this corporate joy by welcoming and acknowledging the Lord's presence at all times, that enabled us to live in the 'yet'. In some versions of this scripture we read 'in spite of', 'despite' or 'nevertheless'. As a pastor, as a congregation and as a community, my Iraqi Christian family and I learned to live in Habakkuk's 'yet': we learned to maintain the attitude of 'nevertheless'. We understood and experienced the reality of the Lord's presence alone being 'fullness of joy', and this reality sustained us through times of great turmoil. Though we were persecuted, though we could hear the sounds of missiles, bomb explosions and gunfire, though we saw trauma, though we witnessed bloodshed, violence and hatred, yet we were joyful in God our Saviour. This is a lesson to all of us; we must all learn that there is a 'despite', a 'nevertheless', in which we can steady our hearts during times of fear, challenge and lack.

Finally, one of my favourite verses in the whole of Scripture is the statement made by Habakkuk in his conclusion to this oracle:

The Sovereign LORD is my strength;
he makes my feet like the feet of a deer,
he enables me to tread on the heights.

Both spiritually and physically this verse gives me profound delight. Throughout my entire work and ministry, I have known him to be the God who strengthens, energizes, lifts and elevates. The feet of deer are said to be anatomical wonders in terms of the high keratin content of their hooves, which makes them strong and resistant to cracks, and their powerful hind leg muscles add strength, speed and agility. When I think of these three features – strength, speed and agility – they were the three qualities that I most needed to possess during my work in a war zone. I constantly felt God enabling me in terms of physical stamina, spiritual and emotional energy and mental sharpness to step into the fullness of his strength. In times of persecution I often felt him lift me from the valley of illness, sorrow and fatigue to tread upon the heights.

Prayer

Father, like Habakkuk we say that we 'stand in awe of your deeds' and we pray that you 'repeat them in our day, in our time make them known'.

We pray that we will hear your voice clearly in our time, so that we know the reality of your joy in every situation. As we rejoice in your greatness, let us receive renewed strength and vitality. Amen.

14

To set the captives free

The Spirit of the Sovereign Lord is on me, because the
Lord has anointed me to proclaim good news to the poor.
He has sent me to bind up the broken-hearted, to proclaim
freedom for the captives and release from darkness for the
prisoners.
(Isaiah 61.1)

One of the key messianic passages in the book of Isaiah is the call
to set the captives free. To a certain degree, all of us participating
in the Christian life are engaged in setting captives free. Our call
and ministry involve helping move others from darkness to light,
liberating people spiritually.

It took a while before I realized that working to liberate real captives, people who had been kidnapped, would be at the very heart of
my work. It all started with the siege of the Church of the Nativity
in Bethlehem (see Chapters 6 and 7). Back then, I thought that the
39 days of negotiation seemed like for ever. Little did I know that
the time would come when I would be negotiating for the release of
my own friends and bodyguards.

In any situation where you are working for the return of hostages, you always need to be aware that this work – setting the captives free – is indeed the work of the kingdom of God. It also needs
to happen very quickly. I have worked on 159 kidnapping cases,
and I have helped release only 49 people – but that is 49 more than
most others involved in this kind of work: a 31 per cent success
rate. There are several major international commercial companies
that charge a huge amount of money to resolve hostage situations.
Sometimes they are successful.

In all of these cases, time is of the essence. If you don't manage to get the person back in a few days, the reality is you have probably moved into a very long-term situation, one that is likely to last for weeks, months or years. I remember every case I have worked on. The joy experienced on somebody's return is simply immense; the pain when somebody is killed is more than devastating and has always driven me to tears.

During my later years in Iraq we met every week as a hostage negotiating team in the US Embassy. The team consisted of staff from the CIA and FBI, and from military intelligence, and together we discussed each case and my role. In private, I prayed and prayed; often those who came to chapel gathered together on Sundays and prayed for wisdom and success.

The first thing you have to do in any kidnap situation is ascertain who is most likely to have committed this crime. The more you know about the 'bad guys', the more likely you are to be able to determine what kind of things they are looking for. If a ransom is wanted, it is immediately considered a simpler case. The more complex situations are those where there is a more political requirement. These cases have included demands by extremist groups for the release of a major terrorist from prison, or for control over a key government decision. This form of negotiation always requires hours of talks with high-ranking government officials, as well as senior religious leaders with influence over these different groups.

In our work, we have never paid money to known terrorist groups, yet in reality, in the early days just after the 2003 war, some people were kidnapped simply because their captors wanted to make money quickly. If you got money to them, you would get the kidnapped victim back. If you did not, they would kill him or her. Often in such circumstances, the families of the victims desperately wanted to pay the ransom money, but they did not know to whom and how to pay it.

The amount to be paid for foreigners was always millions of American dollars, as opposed to just thousands for local people.

I remember one early case when some European staff of a prominent non-governmental organization (NGO) were taken.

The bad guys immediately came to us and told us exactly what they wanted. It did not take long before people realized that I was the one they needed.

We were well acquainted with the ambassador who represented the country the NGO workers were from, and the country in question had a clear public policy of not paying ransoms. We discussed the options frankly with the ambassador: 'You pay, you get them back alive: you don't, they will be killed.' That was the stark choice. The ambassador clearly knew that the only option was to pay. We then negotiated a reduction in the price, from $20 million to $10 million. We collected the money in cash, and Dawood, my unofficial adopted son, drove the money to the bad guys, and we got the people back. The government concerned made a huge deal of its triumph in rescuing its people. Of course, its officials continued to insist they did not pay ransoms.

Another kidnapping case I worked long and hard on was to rescue not Iraqis or Westerners, but Brazilian security staff. A lot of security workers at that time were South Americans because they were much cheaper to employ than American or British staff. The South American personnel had all been soldiers in their own countries, and had experience in dealing with kidnappings. After a lot of effort, it became clear which group of dubious characters was most likely to be involved in this crime. I decided to go and find them. My team knew that I was going, but because confidentiality was critical to the success of the mission, I did not disclose the details to anyone other than my driver, who was also one of my bodyguards. My other bodyguards drove in a separate vehicle behind us, but only up to a certain point, after which I proceeded towards the location alone with my driver.

I found the 'bad guys' in a dangerous and distant suburb of Baghdad. They clearly did not want to talk and immediately pushed my arms behind my back and led me to a derelict outhouse. They then opened the padlocked door and threw me inside, and I fell on to a hard floor. I was now in essence kidnapped too, and locked in a totally black room, with no light. I could do nothing and see nothing. This was the reality of coming to set the captives free.

The passage from Isaiah above also speaks about release from darkness; now I was in real darkness. I suddenly remembered that my captors had not confiscated my phone. There was no signal where I was, so I could not call anybody, but I used the light on the phone to look at where I had been thrown. I could see that, all over the floor, there were severed fingers and toes. I remember praying, 'Please, not my fingers, Lord.'

In those early days I always travelled with large amounts of emergency money strapped to my waist. My captors had not found this either. Also on the phone, I had music by Roni, the dear child of my friends the Shavits, who was born on the day Caroline and I were married. Roni is one of the finest pianists I have ever met, and so I took the risk and listened to some of her music. I was inspired to pray to set the captives free and for light. Now I was the captive in darkness.

The next morning my captors appeared. I was so nice to them. I told them I respected them, and that if they drove me away from there, I would tell nobody where they were and would give them my secret supply of money. My sweet talk and money worked.

The sad reality is that the Brazilian hostages had already been killed by the people who took me hostage. Their bodies were never discovered, but it is highly likely that the fingers and toes were theirs.

Thank God I was free, but now I knew what it was like to actually be kidnapped for a short time. I also knew about the direct intervention of the Almighty in setting the captives free. He may not be setting you free from being kidnapped, but he *is* setting you free to do the work of his kingdom.

Prayer

Lord, who are the captives you are asking us to free? Who are those you want us to liberate?

Lord, we thank you that you always show us your ways. We thank you for the light you give us in our darkness. Thank you, Lord, that you are here. Amen.

15

To Hebron we go

Abraham lived a hundred and seventy-five years. Then Abraham breathed his last and died at a good old age, an old man and full of years; and he was gathered to his people. His sons Isaac and Ishmael buried him in the cave of Machpelah near Mamre, in the field of Ephron son of Zohar the Hittite, the field Abraham had bought from the Hittites. There Abraham was buried with his wife Sarah. After Abraham's death, God blessed his son Isaac, who then lived near Beer Lahai Roi.

(Genesis 25.7–11)

Central to so much of my work in the Holy Land is my love for the city of Hebron.

The town's name comes from a root-verb in Hebrew meaning 'to join', and means 'covenant', 'alliance', 'friendship' or 'society'. It is a place of great historical significance. Abraham dwelt there, and it was here that God changed his name from Abram to Abraham. Hebron was later set apart as a place for the Levites to dwell, and subsequently became a 'city of refuge'.[1] Finally it was the place where David was anointed king. As such, it was in former times known for being a place of divine encounter, protection, community and kingship.

Today Hebron should be a place of unity where Jews, Christians and Muslims come together in the final resting place of the great

---

1 The 'cities of refuge' were six Levitical towns in the kingdom of Israel and the kingdom of Judah in which the perpetrators of accidental manslaughter could claim the right of asylum.

patriarch Abraham – the holy shrine of the father of Judaism and Islam which is known as the Machpelah. We might have hoped that it would be a centre of reconciliation and unity, but sadly Hebron has instead been a focus of great hostility and division. It is a dark location which has seen many acts of aggression between Jews and Muslims.

One major historical event that will always be remembered is simply known as the 'massacre of Hebron'. It happened during the British Mandate in 1929 when 69 Jews were killed in one day in a Palestinian revolt, a terrible incident that has never been forgotten in the region.

Over the years many other dreadful events of violence occurred, but a particular atrocity that scars Israeli history was the shocking massacre committed by Dr Baruch Goldstein. On 25 February 1994, Goldstein, an Israeli-American physician from the Hebron settlement of Kiryat Arba, opened fire on Muslim worshippers at Abraham's shrine. At least 29 people were killed in this massacre and over 125 others were badly injured.

The grave site of Dr Goldstein became a place of pilgrimage for extremist Israeli settlers. The Israeli government reacted to the radical settler groups such as Kach, a group led by Rabbi Meir Kahane, by criminalizing them and banning even the regular settlers from having anything to do with these extremists.

Sadly, we see how the shrine of our great patriarch has become an emblem of terror, not healing; of division, not reconciliation and community. For us, Hebron has become a major place of challenge for our ministry of reconciliation. It reminds us of the dangers of 'religion gone wrong'. But, I believe, if wrong religion is the cause of the problems, then right religion and faith, under the inspiration of the Holy Spirit, is also the only cure for the brokenness and division that seep through the region as if from an open wound.

As I think of Hebron, I think of the challenges we continue to confront, not least in our churches. Are they not all meant to be locations of God's holy covenant – places resembling the biblical Hebron where, like Abraham, the lonely can find a home and encounter a God able to change their name, restore and redefine them, and call them from their past into a new future? Are they not to be places of anointing and kingdom unity, places of priestly purity and refuge for the hurting?

Yet these modern-day 'Hebrons' have so often departed radically from their original design and function, divided and ripped apart by people who think that only their way is acceptable. The challenge to all of us is to follow the way of humility. One of the biggest lessons I have learned in my years working as a peacemaker is that we cannot move forward unless we are willing to make compromises. So often, we think that if we make compromises we are not holding to the truth. What we cannot and must not do is make compromises in our faith in the Almighty, but it is a different matter when it comes to our relationships with others in our worshipping communities. The verb 'compromise' simply means 'to make a promise together', for two parties to make a proposal or put forward an agreement. In this sense, when I see people who within all of their political and religious differences promise to work together for peace, I see mutual love and unity develop.

As we see in the scripture from Genesis above, those who would in time become the leaders of the Jews and Muslims came together in unity to bury their father Abraham. It is within this context that we find the place of harmony: a compromise, a promise to work together and a level of reconciliation.

To this day Jews and Muslims are still divided, and a significant part of our organization continues to seek ways to promote peace and call for reconciliation. One of the associations we work with is the 'Isaac and Ishmael project' that we established with Pastor Steven Khoury from Bethlehem. This work aims to meet the real needs of Jews, Christians and Muslims anywhere in the land of the Holy One. It is wonderful that together we can seek to bring healing and hope to broken people of all faith traditions. The Jews of southern Israel could not believe it when our team of Palestinian Christians first started to take relief to them when they were being shelled by Hamas in Gaza. At the heart of the priestly call that

I mentioned in relation to Hebron is the call to provide help and refuge to those who are suffering.

There has been much debate recently as to whether followers of Islam and Christianity worship the same God. In our Scriptures there are clear links with the God of Abraham, Isaac and Jacob. However, for us, as Christians, central to our faith is the person of Jesus of Nazareth, born in Bethlehem, accepted by many as Jesus the Messiah, the anointed one of God. He was Jewish, and was first accepted by many Jews who became his followers. Even today, in the promised land and around the world, there is a significant number of Jews who still see Jesus as their Messiah. These Jews call themselves either 'Jewish believers' or 'Messianic Jews'. Both terms can be offensive to Jews, however, as all religious Jews would see themselves as 'believing' Jews, and most observant Jews do believe in the coming of the Mashiach (Messiah). As we go forward, we need to see tolerance and understanding from both sides.

I first started going to Hebron in the days of Sheikh Tal al-Sadr, who was from the main Palestinian part of Hebron and one of the key leaders of the original Alexandria Declaration. This was an agreement signed on 21 January 2002. It marked the first occasion when Jews, Christians and Muslims came together to declare their need to work alongside one another for peace, based on their belief in and love of God. Not long after the signing of this historic declaration, Sheikh Tal al-Sadr became very ill and eventually died. Michael Melchior, a chief rabbi, attended the funeral. At that time, he was part of the Israeli government and therefore not allowed to visit the Arab part of the city. But he was so committed to the reality of the role of love in peacemaking that he was prepared to take great risks and show in a practical way his love and respect for the 'other' there in Hebron, the place whose very name speaks of unity and friendship.

Today the Machpelah, the tomb of the patriarchs, is known more for division than unity. There are days that are set aside for the Jews to visit and days set aside for the Muslims, but sadly there are no days when they are both there together. Just down the road from the shrine is Kiryat Arba (Town of the Four), a modern new town which is a vibrant Jewish settlement. Unfortunately, the two have no engagement with each other.

Hebron should be a real place of reconciliation. Both in the town itself and in modern-day Hebrons all over the world, in our places of worship and encounter, we should establish our people in covenant love and harmony of purpose and identity. As King David assures us, 'Behold, how good and pleasant it is when brothers dwell in unity!' (Psalm 133.1 ESV).

So often, even our Christian centres are places of conflict and division, and sadly it is often only in tragedy that people really come together in unity. We too must be driven by passion to come together and stay together. The pain of broken worshipping communities is so real and so deep. Let us be mindful of our heritage and remember to pray for peace and harmony.

Prayer

Heavenly Father, as we look at the story of Hebron, we are fraught with pain to see such division where there should be unity. Lord, we pray that where there is conflict, even in our places of worship, you will cause us to be radical in our search for peace. May your peace sustain us; for Lord, you are here and your Spirit is with us. Amen.

16

I have seen the Lord

Then Job replied to the LORD . . .
'You said, "Listen now, and I will speak; I will question you,
and you shall answer me." My ears had heard of you but now
my eyes have seen you. Therefore I despise myself and repent
in dust and ashes.'
(Job 42.1–6)

During my time in Iraq I went regularly to al-Kifl, the place of
Ezekiel's shrine between Babylon and Najaf. On the return journey
to Baghdad I would always see in the distance another shrine,
located in-between Babylon and Baghdad. This shrine looked more
significant than the one at al-Kifl. I would often ask the soldiers
driving me what exactly the place was and they would simply tell
me it was a shrine. After several months of passing this site, I said to
my soldiers that we really must go over and investigate it. As we did,
we observed that it was a very grand place; not in the grand style
of Najaf, Karbala or Kadhimiya, the main Shia shrines in Iraq, but
very handsome nonetheless.

I eventually spoke to the main imam there, and to my total surprise I found that it was the shrine to Ayyub. Ayyub is none other
than Job. At this stage I was not aware that Job was taken seriously
in Islam. I knew that he came from Uz, in Iraq, but I did not know
that he was revered there. In fact, there are 25 prophets in Islam, of
whom Ayyub is one, though not in the front rank like Abraham,
David and Moses. Ayyub is seen as a great worshipper; a man who,
though suffering much, never stopped worshipping his God.

The story in the Qur'an is very similar to the biblical story,
yet also very different. Ayyub is described as a descendant of Noah,

in a direct line from Esau the son of Ishaq (Isaac). Of the 25 prophets in Islam, at least 14 lived in Iraq/Mesopotamia and the others lived in Israel.

In the Bible, Job is seen as one of the great messengers of hope and peace. He knew profound suffering on every level, yet he never once turned his back on God, his lover and creator. To us, the book of Job, this great poem, is a work of theodicy, the branch of theology that defends divine goodness and justice in the face of the existence of evil. One asks oneself: how can a God of love allow evil acts against humanity to take place? The author of the book of Job deals with the true story of many of our lives. How can a God of love allow such evil?

As I go about my life here in the Middle East, when so many people I love have been killed and kidnapped, I am continually faced with the question, 'How can your loving God allow these things?' I have no easy answers other than that the true solution to every form of death and destruction is love. The totality of love, I believe, is the essence of God the Father and the expression of those who choose to manifest his divine love. I pray that as destruction, despair and carnage continue, we will grow in our awareness that our Lord is always standing beside us in the storm.

During some of our darkest moments, when several of our children from the community were beheaded by ISIS[1] for refusing to convert to Islam and for speaking of their faith in Yeshua (Jesus), two of our girls (who are now teenagers in the school we established for them in Jordan) had the same dream: they saw their slaughtered friends dancing with Jesus in heaven.

May all of us, even in moments and seasons of trial and despair, experience a place of revelation and encounter so that, like Job, we are always able to say, 'Before, I had heard of you, O Lord, but now I have seen you with my own eyes.' My Iraqi children had heard of him, and had even seen his angels, but now in the depths of their sleep they were seeing him.

---

1 The common acronym for the terrorist organization known as the Islamic State in Iraq and Syria; also known as the Islamic State in Iraq and the Levant (ISIL).

Yes, prayer does work, even though it may take a long time. God never fails.

Persistence in prayer and acts of faith is never easy, but it always bears results. As I say time and time again, the Lord is here and his Spirit is with us.

> Then Job replied to the LORD:
> 'I know that you can do all things; no purpose of yours can be thwarted. You asked, "Who is this that obscures my plans without knowledge?" Surely I spoke of things I did not understand, things too wonderful for me to know.'
> (Job 42.1–3)

There really is no greater encouragement in our suffering than reading the book of Job and holding on to those wonderful final words: 'Before, I had heard of you, O Lord, but now I have seen you with my own eyes.' Once we have seen the Lord, we will never be the same again. It is often in our intense pain that we will eventually see the vision and reality of God with us. As in Job 42.5, we also can say, 'My ears had heard of you but now my eyes have seen you.'

Prayer

Lord, O Lord, our God, like your dear Son Jesus, like your prophet Job, we have known pain and brokenness. May we, like Job, be able to say, 'Before, I had heard of you, O Lord, but now I have seen you with my own eyes.'

Thank you, Lord, that you are here and your Spirit is with us. Amen.

17

The number seven

By the seventh day God had finished the work he had been doing; so on the seventh day he rested from all his work. Then God blessed the seventh day and made it holy, because on it he rested from all the work of creating that he had done.
(Genesis 2.2–3)

Since childhood the number seven has always been very significant to me. All biblical numbers have divine symbolic significance and, for me, seven is at the heart of my faith.

When we look at the six days of the creation account, we see the perfection and completeness of the number seven and how it relates to divine perfection. The seventh day was the day of rest, the day on which our divine creator contemplated his creative work.

The number seven lies at the very heart of the Jewish understanding of the non-Jew. Judaism is not a faith of conversion and does not preach that one needs to be Jewish to gain salvation. It does, however, teach that there are seven basic rules that must be obeyed for non-Jews to gain salvation. Those rules are known as the Sheva Mitzvot Bnei Noach (the seven laws of the children of Noah). It may appear strange to include a section on the Noahide laws in a Christian meditation, but in truth these laws align very closely with the foundation values of the Christian faith.

Among the members of the Orthodox Hasidic community, I will often hear them discussing me in Yiddish and saying that I am a 'Noahide', in other words that I am as near to them as I can get and will ever be.

The Orthodox Hasidic Jews teach that soon after creation, God gave seven simple rules that the children of Noah had to observe to return to God. These seven rules became known as the Universal Moral Laws. They were laws that all people of belief in God would want to follow.

These seven Noahide *mitzvot* are simply:

1 Acknowledge that there is only one God, who is infinite and supreme above all things. Do not replace that Supreme Being with finite idols, be it yourself or other beings.
2 Honour the Creator.
3 Value human life. Every human being is essentially an entire world. To save a life is to save that entire world. To destroy a life is to destroy an entire world. To help others live is a corollary of this principle.
4 Respect the institution of marriage. Marriage is a divine covenantal act. The marriage of a man and a woman is a reflection of the oneness of God and his creation. Disloyalty in marriage is an assault on that oneness.
5 Respect the rights and property of others. Be honest and righteous in all your business dealings, and honour God as the provider of life.
6 Respect God's creatures. At first, human beings were forbidden to consume meat. After the Great Flood they were permitted – but with a warning: do not cause unnecessary suffering to any creature.
7 Maintain justice. Justice is God's business, but we are given the charge to lay down necessary laws and enforce them whenever we can. When we right the wrongs of society, we are acting as partners in the act of sustaining creation.

While these laws are not explicitly mentioned in the Bible, the concepts on which they are based are completely biblical and in complete harmony with the Torah.

Just as the seven days of creation are technically six, the seven Noahide laws are really only six, because the first is not a law, but rather an acknowledgement of the presence of the living God Almighty. It is not a law that one believes in and acts on; instead it underlies the laws that follow, and it is more fundamental than all the other commands – just like the first of the Ten Commandments, which simply requires us to acknowledge that the true God is one: 'I am the Lord your God. You shall not have any gods before me.' Both the first commandment and the first Noahide *mitzvah* simply acknowledge the unity and oneness of God.

The 'seven' that is the most fundamental to my work and ministry is the sevenfold nature of the Holy Spirit:

> The Spirit of the LORD shall rest upon him, the Spirit of wisdom and understanding, the Spirit of counsel and might, the Spirit of knowledge and the fear of the LORD. And his delight shall be in the fear of the LORD.
> (Isaiah 11.2–3 ESV)

The Spirit of the Lord, and the spirits of wisdom, of understanding, of counsel, of might, of knowledge and of fear of the Lord are the seven spirits which are before the throne of God.

These seven spirits are often presented in the shape of the menorah, the seven-branched candlestick (see Figure 2). These are

Figure 2 **The menorah –
the seven-branched candlestick
of Judaism**
(Copyright © Getty Images, adapted)

seen as the same seven spirits who are before the throne of Jesus mentioned in the New Testament book of Revelation. The central upright of the menorah is often seen as the Spirit of the Lord, the fullness of the one who brings freedom, sets the captives free and announces jubilee. Thus, once again, as with the days of creation where the seventh is a consummation point and all about God, so the same may be said about the Spirit of the Lord.

Just as there are many facets, dimensions and names for God and for Jesus, so there are many dimensions to the Holy Spirit. Very often during my work and ministry, I have been aware of each of these aspects ('personas') of the Holy Spirit assisting me and my people, guiding and directing me, illuminating my path and breathing on my worshipping congregation at St George's.

For example, in important political and executive decisions involving high levels of risk-taking, I often felt the Holy Spirit giving me godly wisdom and counsel, even during the night hours. I learned that 'risk-taking' and 'wisdom' are not mutually exclusive, and that one can be a 'wise and reflective risk-taker'. One only has to look at Scripture to see that wisdom and prudence can actually 'help' us to take risks when we are attuned to God's voice speaking through his Spirit. Risk-taking in God's kingdom is not about heading mindlessly into danger, nor is it about being rash or impulsive; it is about listening to the spirits of wisdom and counsel which enable one to see from a higher perspective. When risks need to be taken, the presence of God always resources me with courage and strength and peace, even in the most dangerous of situations.

The spirit of might is an aspect of the Holy Spirit that has been extremely evident in my life, not simply in terms of the energy and stamina required by anyone in full-time ministry, but also in terms of the physically exhausting nature of much of my work. The health challenges that I have faced have never prevented me from doing what God has called me to do, and the divine 'enablement' that I have experienced has been due to the Spirit of Might, the energy of God's Spirit rising up in my body and soul. Even during times when I felt desperately ill and weak, the Holy Spirit has fortified me and carried me through. He is the one who gives strength beyond all strength.

The spirit of knowledge has so often given me a sense of 'knowing' and 'predicting' outcomes deep inside me, enabling me to act and make decisions out of divine intuition rather than just good ideas. Often, in highly dangerous situations, this has resulted in many lives being preserved, including my own. It is simple enough to say that without the full manifest presence of the Holy Spirit in my work, I would never have achieved what I did achieve.

Whether I was involved in negotiating the freedom of hostages, visiting prisoners or dealing with presidents and prime ministers, the spirit of understanding has often accelerated and sharpened much of the insight required.

And, over all, the reverent fear of the Lord has enabled me never to step into a position of moral compromise on any level.

Whatever our place of work, and whatever situation we find ourselves in, we must rely on the Holy Spirit in all of his fullness so that we live a life that optimizes and does not minimize the supernatural presence of God. Only when we do this can we truly live out the great call that has been set before us all and exemplified by Jesus:

> The Spirit of the Sovereign LORD is on me, because the LORD has anointed me to proclaim good news to the poor. He has sent me to bind up the broken-hearted, to proclaim freedom for the captives and release from darkness for the prisoners. (Isaiah 61.1; see also Luke 4.18)

The next really important 'seven' in my life comes right at the end of the Christian Bible, in John's letter to the seven churches in Revelation. To these seven churches that have experienced the love of Jesus, he has seven very different lessons. Each letter involves warnings and exhortations, all of which are relevant to us today:

1 *Ephesus (Revelation 2.1–7).* The church that had forsaken its first love (2.4).

2 *Smyrna (Revelation 2.8–11).* The church that would suffer persecution (2.10).

3 *Pergamum (Revelation 2.12–17).* The church that needed to repent (2.16).

4 *Thyatira (Revelation 2.18–29).* The church that had a false prophet (2.20).

5 *Sardis (Revelation 3.1–6).* The church that had fallen asleep (3.2).

6 *Philadelphia (Revelation 3.7–13).* The church that had endured patiently (3.10).

7 *Laodicea (Revelation 3.14–22).* The church with a lukewarm faith (3.16).

These churches were all presented with hard messages. Five of them were seriously failing in their calling, to such an extent that one of them – Laodicea – was seen as being lukewarm.

My favourite of the churches is clearly the one in Smyrna. This is the church with which my community in the Middle East most clearly identifies: the persecuted church. In the second century the celebrated Polycarp, a pupil of the apostle John, was a highly prominent leader in the church of Smyrna. Here he suffered martyrdom, in AD 155. The name itself, Smyrna, is likely to have derived from the Ancient Greek word for 'myrrh', which relates so much to suffering and death:

And to the angel of the church in Smyrna write: 'The words of the first and the last, who died and came to life.

'I know your tribulation and your poverty (but you are rich) and the slander of those who say that they are Jews and are not, but are a synagogue of Satan. Do not fear what you are about to suffer. Behold, the devil is about to throw some of you into prison, that you may be tested, and for ten days you will have tribulation. Be faithful unto death, and I will give you the crown of life. He who has an ear, let him hear what the Spirit says to the churches. The one who conquers will not be hurt by the second death.'
(Revelation 2.8–11 ESV)

This passage gives hope to the persecuted Church around the world. Yes, things will be terrible, but for those who remain grateful – for those who are faithful and hold fast to their faith in Father, Son and Spirit – there will be a great heavenly reward. Eternal life is the great gift for those whose allegiance is unshakeable. The exhortation is not to fear but to be aware that God knows exactly what these people are facing. Many will suffer greatly; they may be thrown into prison and become seriously tested to the end (as we have seen, both with adult and child martyrs). Yet fear cannot conquer real love, and the best is yet to come. As we know from the wonderful exhortation of the apostle Paul to the Romans: 'The sufferings of this present world are not worthy to be compared with the glory that is to come' (Romans 8.18, paraphrased).

Prayer

Lord God, our master and maker of all, we thank you that you have not left us without direction. We thank you for the sevenfold Holy Spirit and that the suffering now is nothing to be compared with the glory that is to come. Amen.

18
No, never alone

Be strong and courageous. Do not be afraid or terrified because
of them, for the LORD your God goes with you; he will never
leave you nor forsake you.
(Deuteronomy 31.6)

When we look at Scripture, we Christians often believe that
all the verses that give us encouragement and hope come from
the New Testament. But as you will see from this book, so much
of my vision, hope, courage and strength comes from the Hebrew
Scriptures. Every week I post on social media a short commentary
on the week's Parsha Torah reading, read by Jews around the world.
The Parsha is a section of the Torah that is used in Jewish liturgy
and consists of a specific scriptural focus each week. These readings
always give me great hope and insight, and teach me things that I
have never really grasped.

In our constant journey of life, we are all faced with difficulties
and often confronted by the question: how do we keep going?
We may be struggling with illness, unemployment or bereavement. For me in war zones, it was often a huge struggle when
under enemy attack. I will never forget a typical evening in
Baghdad on Maundy Thursday. We had our service organized in
the US Embassy chapel. We had already had our Iraqi service of
foot-washing at St George's Church – a ritual which Iraqis take
very seriously. We had even talked about service to our enemies
(and we had plenty of them). Now it was to the US Embassy for a
special service there.

Most of our congregation were soldiers. It was far too difficult for
them to take off their boots, so we settled for washing their hands,

and the service began. I had just got into the liturgy when the rockets started blasting towards us. We were in the midst of praise and worship and suddenly everybody, apart from me, fell to the floor. Our worship leader, from his kneeling position on the floor, went on playing the piano. The worship that followed as we sang the song 'No, Never Alone' was the most powerful worship I have ever experienced. I had never heard the song before, though I now realize it is a very popular old gospel hymn:

No, never alone, no, never alone,
He promised never to leave me,
Never to leave me alone.
(Ludie Pickett, 1868-1953)

What powerful words these are, in the midst of battle! The one assurance we have is that we will never be alone, because our Lord, our creator and maker, is with us. Time and time again, even in the midst of the countless disasters of life, we are continually reminded of the eternal presence of God's love. In Deuteronomy, the heart of the Torah, is that promise, given by the Almighty, that he will always be with us. It is a thread of assurance that runs throughout the Bible, clearly present in both the Hebrew Scriptures and the New Testament. Let's read it again: 'Be strong and courageous. Do not be afraid or terrified because of them, for the LORD your God goes with you; he will never leave you nor forsake you.'

It is indeed only when we truly believe in the Almighty and follow him with all our heart that we can truly be the strong and courageous people we are called to be. Once again this is true for us not just when we live in the midst of terror, but wherever we are called to serve the Almighty. He promises us his constant presence, his undying attention and concern.

Jesus himself shared the same message – that his followers would never be alone – when he said, 'Go therefore and make disciples of all the nations . . . and lo, I am with you always, even to the end of the age' (Matthew 28.19-20 NKJV).

So the message of Jesus is in line with that of his Father: simply that we are indeed never alone. There are great expectations on us who follow Jesus, but there is also great provision for us. We have been given the assurance of the ever-abiding presence of the Almighty. It may seem at times as if God is far away, but his eternal assurance and promise to us is simply this: 'Never will I leave you; never will I forsake you' (Hebrews 13.5).

So the rockets and mortars may have been attacking us. Everything may seem so bad in our life, but the promise of our Lord is always the same and his perfect love casts out all fear: he will never leave you, and that means that perfect love will not leave you. The events of that service never left me and have never left some of my very good friends from those days. Some of them I see quite frequently, and every time we meet we come back to the song of that night. I have often been preaching in churches in America with people who were with us that evening and the theme has regularly come up time and time again. He is faithful and he is true. Whatever dangerous situation I have ever faced since that day, I always end up singing the words of that old gospel hymn:

No, never alone, no, never alone,
He promised never to leave me,
Never to leave me alone.

It is this simple yet profound message that has always been with me throughout my journey of faith, life and mission, and continues to resonate in my heart today. So do not be afraid. The Lord is near, and so often he fights our battles for us. Keep worshipping him, and the more you do, the more aware you will become of his presence.

Prayer

Thank you for your promise, Lord. May I hold on to it at all times, regardless of what is going on around me. Lord, we do indeed thank you that we are never alone. Amen.

19
Why, Lord, why?

Why, LORD, do you stand far off?
Why do you hide yourself in times of trouble?
(Psalm 10.1)

There are times when all us have to ask the question, 'Why, Lord, why?' Like so many questions in our life, there are rarely answers to this cry. Yet, even in the midst of such darkness, we know the Lord is always with us.

My story is a story of two lands, Israel and Iraq, and there have been times when the two have almost miraculously come together. I have mentioned already my long association with the bone marrow transplant unit in Baghdad. There was a very high incidence of paediatric leukaemia in the area, which was believed to be linked to the depleted uranium that covered many of the weapons dropped in Operation Desert Storm in 1990.

One of the key Iraqi generals working with the Coalition Provisional Authority following the 2003 war was General Nashbandi. He became a good friend and one day he came to me with a serious concern. He had a three-year-old grandson, Suheil, who was very ill with leukaemia. The haematology unit was convinced that he had a serious chance of being cured, if only he could have a bone marrow transplant. This was impossible in Iraq, so General Nashbandi asked whether I could arrange it.

The nearest option was Israel, so I began intense discussions with the medical staff of Hadassah University in Jerusalem. After much negotiation, it was agreed that they would proceed with treatment. The Nashbandi family, like all Iraqis, had only heard bad things about Israel and the 'evil Zionists'. Yet General Nashbandi, the grandfather, remembered the good things about the Iraqi Jews from the past. He remembered how clever, courageous and hard-working they were and how they could innovate, pioneer and achieve what others could not. Thus he was in full support of his grandson going to Israel to be treated. As usual I offered to find the money needed to make the venture happen. The hospital was very supportive, and eventually Suheil arrived.

He was suffering a lot and the journey had been hard for him, but at least there was hope. We had to be very quiet about the venture; it was extremely difficult raising money for anybody going from Iraq to Israel, even for life-saving treatment. Nothing could be said publicly. Support came from some Jewish friends, the hospital itself helped hugely, and most of the doctors donated their time free of charge. The family could not believe the amount of care and love that was shown to them by these supposedly evil Israelis.

The procedure was not easy. First, Suheil had to go through serious chemotherapy before the harvested bone marrow from his mother could be implanted. There were many risks. He responded very well at the beginning, but then developed life-threatening infections. We prayed and prayed so hard for him, but it became clear there was no more that could be done, and dear little Suheil died.

There was another time I desperately cried out for help, when a seven-year-old girl in our congregation, Rita, was ill. She had a rare form of bladder cancer, and the treatment that could be provided for her in Iraq was very limited. Each Sunday she would come to church and kneel in the middle of the sanctuary. Every time I saw her, I would pray for her and anoint her. I prayed so hard for her healing and knew that without a miracle we would need to find a way to treat her. A new member of the US Embassy congregation turned out to be a urologist who specialized in treating the very kind of bladder tumour that Rita had. We took her to see him, and although he could not treat her, he knew a surgeon who could do this in Jordan. We gathered all the funds together for her medical care.

We finally got the family to Jordan. They were a big family so they all came. The hospital decided they needed to completely remove Rita's bladder. This they did and the operation was very successful. However, it was only a few weeks before she lost the sight in one of her eyes. It looked very much as if she had a secondary tumour, and this was soon confirmed by a CAT scan.

I loved Rita so much. She started to rapidly go downhill. All I could do was love her and hold her. I prayed for her every day and anointed her. I still had to be in Iraq as well, so I would travel back and forth to be with her. One night when I was in Iraq, I had a call that Rita was now in a deep coma. I went back to Jordan as quickly as I could, but by the time I got there, she had died.

There are no words to describe what I felt. There were no words to describe what Rita's family felt. I wish I had some good uplifting words to say in this meditation but I don't. This chapter has been so difficult for me to write due to the pain of remembering, but at least I know that Rita is with Jesus. I wrote to my friend Sonia in Hong Kong and told her how difficult it was. She herself had lost one of her babies and she said the only thing she could hold on to in the Bible was the shortest verse in Scripture: 'Jesus wept' (John 11.35).

I used to be based at Coventry Cathedral, which had a project called 'Remember Our Child' as a central part of its ministry. It was a ministry that remembered the children people had lost. Losing a child is a continual agony. Yes, he or she is out of suffering and with our Lord, but you cannot pretend that the pain will go. All you can know is that, in the midst of the pain, the Lord is there crying with you.

I had to organize Rita's funeral. I have done very many funerals, including for my father, my brother and other relatives, but nothing was like this one. It was simply the hardest service I have ever taken, and even in the service there were periods when I just could not stop crying. All I could do was say, 'Why, Lord? Why?'

As I went through this pain, the only hope I had was that I have a God who also suffered, who also wept when his dear friend Lazarus was no more. I realized I was experiencing just a small fraction of what my dear heavenly Father had suffered when his

Son had died. My Rita, my unofficial adopted daughter . . . So many of my children in Iraq saw me as their father and still do. Although most of them are now married and several have children, as adults they still call me 'Abouna', which means 'Daddy'. I have baptized five of the next generation of children; these little ones all know me as 'Jeddu' (Grandad).

Writing this was so hard, but God has been through immense pain himself and is acquainted with our sorrows. I know that my Rita is with him and free of pain. Since this terrible experience, I have had a new radical allegiance to those who have lost their own child. I stay in contact with her family almost every day, and this relationship gives us all strength and hope. I still say, 'Why, Lord, why?' and he still says, 'I am there.'

Prayer

Why, Lord, why is there such pain and heartache? There are no words easily expressed of comfort and joy. The one thing I know is that Jesus wept. The one thing I know is that you suffer with us, so I say 'Come, Lord Jesus, come.'

I thank you that soon you will come, Lord. Amen.

20

Remember the Sabbath, to keep it holy

Remember the Sabbath day by keeping it holy. Six days you shall labour and do all your work, but the seventh day is a sabbath to the LORD your God.
(Exodus 20.8-10)

The Sabbath, the seventh day, is the day when, after God had created the world, he rested and instructed everybody else to do so as well.

The Ten Commandments are at the very heart of God's covenant with humanity. The Sabbath is mentioned 151 times in Scripture, and at no time are we told not to keep it. Yes, we are told that the Sabbath is made for us, not us for the Sabbath, but that is because the Sabbath is to be a time of joy and liberation. To keep it holy means to set it apart for God because he is holy. Christians often say to me, 'But we are not under the Jewish law, so aren't we set free from that commandment?'

Are we set free from any of the other ten commandments? Can we murder, commit adultery or steal? Of course not. Well, why do we not take the Sabbath more seriously? That is a complex matter, but I will tell you why it moved from Saturday to Sunday. Why the Sabbath has changed is one of the biggest questions in the history of Christianity, yet it is an issue that is very rarely taken seriously by the Christian leadership throughout the world.

At the very beginning of the Christian faith there was not only a major separation from Judaism; there was also the development of a theology which held that the Church had replaced Israel – what came to be known as 'replacement theology' or 'separationist theology'. Then, in the fourth century AD, Constantine was appointed Roman emperor. He became a Christian and started to set down new policies which would increase the separation between Jews and Christians. The Jewish Sabbath ran from sunset on Friday to sunset on Saturday. However, the Romans had previously worshipped the sun god, and the main day of worship was the first day of the week, which was called Sunday. Their worship was called Mithraism. Many of their cultures and practices were grafted into what became known as Christianity. Many of the principal Christian feasts such as Easter and Christmas were intimately linked to the beliefs and practices of Mithraism.

Following the Mithraist pattern of worship, Sunday, the first day of the week, became the day to which Constantine moved the celebration of the Sabbath. So Sunday, the day of traditional adoration of the sun, became the Christian Sabbath day and was observed by the whole Christian Church until the Seventh-day Adventist movement was developed by Ellen White in the USA around the 1860s. This Church still observes the Sabbath on the traditional Shabbat,[1] the Saturday.

I am a Christian priest; the Christian Sabbath is Sunday, but I disagree with moving the Sabbath to Sunday. Yes, it is part of the Christian tradition, but to me it is wrong and caught up in the whole Christian anti-Judaic polemic. I will observe Sunday as the main Christian day of worship, but it is not the Sabbath and never will be. There are those who say that the first day of the week (Sunday) was observed because it was the day of resurrection. I appreciate this point, but I do not think there is any justification within Scripture for the replacement of the Shabbat.

The Sabbath to me is the Holy Seventh Day set aside for holiness, rest and worship of HaShem (the Name of God). I do my best to keep the Sabbath as a day for focusing on God and on the gathering together of his people. At no place in Scripture – the Old and New Testaments – are there instructions not to keep the real Sabbath.

---

1 Hebrew for 'Sabbath'.

Let us remember the Sabbath. Whenever your time of rest, set it aside and keep it holy. Above all, I believe the words of Jesus that God did indeed make the Sabbath for us and not us for the Sabbath: 'Then he said to them, "The Sabbath was made for man, not man for the Sabbath"' (Mark 2.27).

The Sabbath should be, for all of us, something that is liberating, inspiring, a time of undistracted communion with God and focus on all that he is. This place of rest for the soul is important, not just for me in a turbulent war zone, but for all of us. Whether you acknowledge Saturday or Sunday as your Shabbat, what is vital is that you keep it as your important day set aside for God.

It must be said, however, that the overriding reality for Christian new covenant believers lies not simply in these words of Jesus concerning the Sabbath being made for us, but in the presentation of himself as the ultimate place of true rest. In this truth, we see that while the Sabbath is indeed a defined point within the course of the week, its fullness is actually found in the presence of a person. As Jesus said: 'Come to me, all you who are weary and burdened, and I will give you rest / Come to me, all who labour and are heavy laden, and I will give you rest' (Matthew 11.28 NIV/ESV). If we follow this thought through, we realize that there is an element of Sabbath rest that we can experience as a constant everyday reality, a peace that surpasses the boundaries of assigned days and times. Experiencing this wonderful reality has sustained me throughout my work.

Prayer

Lord, you made the Sabbath for us, not us for the Sabbath. May we truly set aside time for communing with you. May they be periods of liberation, restoration and sanctification, and may we know your presence powerfully during these times. Amen.

21
Taking risks

When he ascended up on high, he led captivity captive, and
gave gifts unto men.
(Ephesians 4.8 kjv)

For over a year I was falsely accused of supporting terrorists
in order to rescue sex slaves from ISIS, and I am glad to confirm
that the case has now been closed. At no point did I ever provide
any finances to a terrorist organization to release the enslaved
from captivity. I did, however, have a few productive situations
where I managed to work towards the release of individuals from
captivity. In order to gain any ability to work with these evil terrorist organizations, one needs to understand the essence of their
fundamental flaws.

So often people say to me, 'All these conflicts in the world are
caused by religion', expecting me, as a religious leader, to passion-
ately refute this assertion. The fact is, I ardently agree that religion is indeed the cause of a great amount of evil and destruction.
As Archbishop William Temple stated during the Second World
War, 'When religion goes wrong it goes very wrong.' This reality is
what we have seen in the rise of so much Islamic terrorism. The root
cause of the issue is not about Islam but about 'Islam gone wrong'.
The question is: why has it gone wrong?

Whenever anyone observes a terrorist individual or group, one
always finds to some degree that there has been an element of loss.
If we look at the whole process in Iraq, we see that the process known
as 'de-Baathification' (the widespread eradication of the Arab
Socialist Ba'ath Party led by Saddam Hussein) directly contributed
to the rise of Islamic terrorism. The results of de-Baathification for

many people were the loss of businesses, loss of investments, loss of family and, ultimately, loss of power. Often these individuals were left homeless without any source of income or *raison d'être*.

During this period, a significant amount of the work that we carried out under the direction of the Coalition Provision Authority (which was under the command of General David Petraeus) involved the provision of resources to those who had suffered great loss during this process of de-Baathification. I worked closely with General Petraeus to form a project known as 'The Sons of Iraq'. This process provided fundamental help to those who had lost everything, and attempted to restore to them a sense of identity and self-worth. As a result, the growth of some of these extremist groups was seriously diminished and there existed a level of hope for reform.

However, when the Coalition Provisional Authority relinquished power in Iraq, this process stopped, and I can remember saying then that 'within one year we will have civil war'. The reality was, it did not take one year but as little as six months for the foundations of ISIS to be established. When this extreme terrorist group carried out many atrocities throughout Iraq, and moved progressively into the Levant (including Syria), we were faced with one of the most dreadful crises. I tried to continue my negotiations with some of the former Baathist leaders, but it was nearly impossible to nego-tiate as they were not willing to talk about reconciliation in any shape or form. All they wanted was to demonstrate their power, and this they tried to do by justifying their stance in accordance with their own interpretation of Islam. Many of their own Islamic leaders, such as Grand Ayatollah al-Sistani and Ayatollah al-Sadr, vehemently opposed the position taken by ISIS/ISIL.

For me, what was particularly concerning was that some of the Islamic leaders with whom I had worked and whom I had supported during the whole de-Baathification crisis turned out be the very same people who were now responsible for a new radical rise of ter-rorism, which included taking many women as sex slaves. These slaves ranged in age from young girls to middle-aged women, and they were mainly from the Yazidi community – a small minority

Iraqi religious group which was commonly condemned by many Muslims because its members refused to say anything bad about Satan. The Yazidi belief is that God is good and Satan is bad. Therefore, there is no reason to antagonize the latter by speaking against him. While Christians and Jews could at least be viewed as 'people of the Book', the Yazidis were seen by many Muslims as one of the most 'evil' religious groups existing within Iraqi society. It was these poor victims of sexual predators and atrocious crimes who were the focus of my rescue attempts. As I have stated already, at no point was I willing to pay money for their redemption. I did, however, locate the ex-Baathist leaders whom I had formerly helped and pleaded with them for their assistance in releasing some of these people. My statement to them was, 'When you needed help, I helped you, so now that I need help, I am asking you to help me.' In a very few cases this approach actually worked, resulting in the successful rescue of certain slaves.

The international community is seriously concerned about the rise of terrorism. Whether we observe terrorist acts in Europe, America or the Middle East, the one common factor is that the perpetrators feel they have ultimately lost power, respect and authority. In the case of extremist Islamic terrorism, they consider that their faith tradition is no longer taken seriously and they feel that they are victims of increasing Islamophobia. Governments and peace activists must thus rise to the major challenge of establishing themselves as peacemakers by considering ways in which they can provide what these radicals are seeking.

That is to say, we must be willing and able to find ways of giving back to these people what they feel has been taken from them and provide them with an authentic sense of purpose and identity, as I had attempted with the former Baathists. We must at least try to give them the assurance that they can play a major part in restoring dignity and vision to their own communities. We cannot deny that there is a major religious dimension to this type of initiative, and yes, when 'religion goes wrong' it goes very wrong indeed, but we must not forget that when 'religion goes right' and is redemptive in nature, it can often be a viable solution to conflict.

At the heart of the Christian message is freedom. It was the reason for the cross, and this alone can achieve the complete liberation of any human being. For me personally, it was the centrality of the call to set the captives free that energized my work. The death, resurrection and Ascension of Jesus was all about the divine rescue of those in bondage: 'When he ascended up on high, he led captivity captive, and gave gifts unto men' (Ephesians 4.8 KJV).

Jesus himself demonstrated unequalled courage in order for humankind to have its relationship with God restored and to receive the great gift of eternal life. He knew he had to give himself up as a sacrifice and that this was ultimately the very reason for his birth, yet his impending death caused him so much pain that he cried to the Father, 'If it be possible, let this cup be taken from me.' Yet he was compelled by love.

For all of us, this is the great high call: to be compelled by love. At various points throughout my work in the Middle East, I asked God to 'withdraw the cup' from me. I did not enjoy the work of trying to recover sex slaves, and at times, attempting to avoid the issue, I cried out to my Lord, 'Is there any way out of this?' I heard him respond, 'You know what I have called you to do', and felt his peace and presence surround me. I knew that 'taking risks' was a major part of my calling, as Lord Coggan had made clear to me so many years before, and this enabled me to act with courage and do what I had to do with the prudence, wisdom and insight that God had granted to me.

Prayer

Lord, it is hard being called to take risks for you, yet we know that you took the greatest risk ever for us. May we be ever willing to take great risks for you, so that through our work, O Lord, we will see your kingdom come.

Lord, in your mercy, let your kingdom come. Amen.

22

They are after me, Lord

Have mercy on me, my God, have mercy on me,
for in you I take refuge.
I will take refuge in the shadow of your wings
until the disaster has passed.
I cry out to God Most High,
to God, who vindicates me.
(Psalm 57.1–2)

Sometimes my cry to God just seems to be, 'They are after me, Lord, they are after me.' Often, the more I do to help people, the more other people seem to be annoyed. Very few people truly realize the dangers and difficulties of being a real peacemaker. Many are largely indifferent to the real consequences of having such a role, when groups such as ISIS place a $357 million bounty on your head (my current value, apparently). These terrorists want peacemakers dead or alive. They are opposed to peace.

Another area of tension arises from Christians who oppose the heart of my work in Israel-Palestine, which is driven by a deep love for Israelis and Palestinians. Either I am seen as loving Israel too much and not caring about the Palestinians, or I am too pro-Palestinian and not sufficiently concerned for Israel. Either way, I can't win. Fundamental to my work is the requirement to love both Israelis and Palestinians, and a lot of people don't like the fact that we do so. Yet the core of our ministry is the gospel message of peace and reconciliation, and I do not believe that Christians who take the side of one group and withhold love from the other have fully grasped the message of the kingdom.

I received a barrage of criticism one day from a person in the audience at Hong Kong University, because he heard me say something positive about the Israeli Defence Force (IDF) at a meeting there. Many people allege that the IDF kills young children and prevents Palestinians from having any freedom. I was simply pointing out that the IDF is one of the most efficient armies in the world but is seen as being anti-Palestinian and against defenceless Palestinian children.

Of course, there is the question of why certain Palestinian extremists are using their children to fight in the first place. I do not think the IDF is perfect, but it is one of the most highly skilled armies in the world today. It is also one of the world's leading resources for dealing with major natural disasters. If there are major earthquakes, hurricanes or floods anywhere in the world, the IDF is there helping.

There are many instances of Palestinian children being induced to stab Israeli soldiers. Defenceless youngsters are often cynically used by terrorists. If these children are caught and shot by the army, they are seen as great martyrs for their faith and the cause. I am in a never-ending battle that can never be won, and all of it is in the name of 'justice'.

Justice is meted out on a totally subjective basis according to the motivations of each group, but true justice will only be seen and established when the sovereignty of God is acknowledged, for his rule is righteousness and justice. Scripture makes clear that these are the very foundation of his throne. Justice is therefore a divine reality, and in the context of godless societies (including democratic ones), it can only be a human ideal. It will always be flawed, limited and insufficient.

Regularly I have cried out to God, 'Have mercy on me, have mercy', and it is indeed only in him that I really take refuge, in the shadow of his wings. You may not have a huge price on your head, but I am sure that many of us are faced with unjustified opposition, or have been attacked for no real reason. Then all we can do is to go under the Lord's wings. Here God is presented in angelic form; rescue is found in the shadow of his wings, where one remains until the disaster has passed. Psalm 91 must become a reality for all of us: the safe place of refuge is in the presence of the Almighty.

Often, in the midst of tension and turbulence, I sit and talk to my heavenly Father and ask him for peace, insight and resolve. If we just ask, we will receive help in a greater way than we could have ever imagined.

Sadly, we cannot deny that there is an increase in international anti-Semitism; therefore, as it stands at the moment, Israel is the safest place for Jews in the world. In many countries the cry of Jewish people is simply, 'They are after me, Lord, they are after me.' I have written a lot on the subject of anti-Semitism. It is a huge topic with a complex political and spiritual background, but so often it would seem that attacking the Jews is the nearest human beings can get to attacking God.

Prayer

Come to my rescue, Lord. Flow like mighty rivers.

Bring your justice, Lord – not human justice but yours, Lord. For you are the King of Glory and in you alone we trust. Amen.

23

The Samaritan woman

When a Samaritan woman came to draw water, Jesus said to her, 'Will you give me a drink?' (His disciples had gone into the town to buy food.)

The Samaritan woman said to him, 'You are a Jew and I am a Samaritan woman. How can you ask me for a drink?' (For Jews do not associate with Samaritans.) . . .

'Sir,' the woman said, 'you have nothing to draw with and the well is deep. Where can you get this living water? Are you greater than our father Jacob, who gave us the well and drank from it himself, as did also his sons and his livestock?'

Jesus answered, 'Everyone who drinks this water will be thirsty again, but whoever drinks the water I give them will never thirst. Indeed, the water I give them will become in them a spring of water welling up to eternal life.'

The woman said to him, 'Sir, give me this water so that I won't get thirsty and have to keep coming here to draw water.' (John 4.7-9, 11-15)

Fundamental to the mission of Jesus was his ministry of love, and at the heart of that ministry was the way he worked with despised and rejected people. These included the Samaritans. They were a much-despised community, despised because they were not seen as real Jews. Nor was their temple seen as a proper place to worship, as it was not the Temple in Jerusalem but was located on Mount Gerizim in Samaria.

When we think of the word 'Samaritans', we may immediately think of three things: the parable of the Good Samaritan; the story of Jesus meeting the woman at the well, which we have just read;

and the Samaritans' helpline, set up for those who are depressed or maybe considering suicide. I think of the real Samaritans, still on Mount Gerizim, whom I regularly visit.

They are a very small group of not more than 700 people. About 300 live in Gerizim and 400 in the Tel Aviv area. They wear turbans and speak Arabic, but they are not Arabs. They worship in their ancient synagogue, and read from Sepher Torah scrolls,[1] but are not Jews. Their books of worship are written in an ancient form of Hebrew and Aramaic, and their language is an ancient form of Hebrew. Outside their community, no one understands what their writings say.

The key period for the development of their faith tradition was the Babylonian exile in the sixth century BC. Even here there are some very varying traditions. There are those who say that some of the Samaritans did not go into exile to Babylon, but were left behind in Israel. Others say their faith tradition developed around the time of the Assyrian exile, when, as exiled Jews, they married Assyrians. On returning to Israel, they were not allowed to live in Jerusalem or to worship in the Temple. Instead they became known as the Samaritans, and moved their temple to Mount Gerizim. Thus they were seen as separating from Judaism nearly 30 centuries ago. When they returned from Babylon, their differences with Judaism were so great they could not be reconciled.

To the Samaritans the most holy place in the world is Gerizim. They say this is where Abraham offered to sacrifice his son Isaac, and where Noah's ark landed after the Great Flood. It is clear that for thousands of years the Samaritans have gathered around Mount Gerizim, and it is here that at Passover a lamb is still sacrificed on their altar – a practice that was abandoned by the Jewish community after the destruction of the Temple in AD 70.

The Samaritan High Priest, Elazar ben-Tsedaka ben-Yitzhaq (1927–2010), claimed to be a direct descendant of Moses' brother Aaron. He said the Samaritans have lived in this land for 3,345 years. His own family dates back in the area for 147 generations. They are

---

1 Sepher Torah scrolls are handwritten copies of the Scriptures.

members of a minority community that consider themselves as both Israelis and Palestinians, and legally they carry three passports: Israeli, Palestinian and Jordanian. As in many of the minority groups in the Middle East, there is a serious risk of inbreeding, with the resulting negative phenomena of congenital diseases. Strangely, the community has more young men than women, and they have therefore welcomed a number of Russian Jews into the community. These Russian Jews have converted to being Samaritans, and the women have married their young men. To this day, there is still animosity between the majority of Jews and Samaritans, so it gives me great joy to be able to work with each group.

Fundamental to my work in the Middle East is serving God in this dynamic place, and part of that is continuing to develop the strong relationships that I have with the Samaritans. My experience with them has very much been like our Lord's experience: 'good', while still offering the challenge to salvation that he, in his love, showed them. As Jesus says to the Samaritan woman: 'The time is coming when we will worship neither on this mountain nor in Jerusalem . . . God is Spirit and his worshippers must worship in the Spirit and truth' (John 4.21– 24, paraphrased).

We look at Jesus and the Samaritan woman and we realize fundamental things about Jesus. He may have been serious about his Judaism, but fundamentally he was a person who held to his understanding of the new covenant.

Jesus and the Samaritan woman enter into deep conversation about water. The conversation moves quickly from physical water to spiritual water – the water of life, eternal life. The woman says she wants that eternal water, but she fails to understand the true spiritual dimension of what is being offered. Jesus was concerned about providing this woman with eternal life.

Here, in this simple story involving our Lord, we see the very essence of what our work is about. There are physical needs – Jesus needed real water. There are spiritual needs – and Jesus moved quickly on to the profoundly spiritual question of the water of life that leads to eternal salvation.

In essence, my work in the Middle East is providing for the two-fold needs of those we are called to serve: physical needs and spiritual life. Wherever we may serve, we are called to provide for the physical needs and the spiritual needs of all people. The very nature of our Lord's ministry is always twofold: to feed the five thousand and also to give eternal life and water that will last for ever.

Prayer

Lord Jesus, we thank you that you always met both the physical and spiritual needs of others. Help us to realize that, as your people, we are also called to do both. We thank you that you promise to always provide all that we need to do your work.

Lord, we love you and thank you for our provision. Amen.

24
Danny Fitzsimons

The light shines in the darkness, and the darkness has not overcome it.
(John 1.5)

I have so many stories of light shining on darkness during my years in Baghdad. However, there are few more memorable than that of my dear friend Danny Fitzsimons. In 2010 I was contacted by his stepmother, who told me the story of her step-son: he had been accused of murder in Baghdad. I was the only person whom his family knew in Baghdad, so they contacted me through the media. They wanted to know if I, as a priest, could get to see him.

I did not believe there was anything I could do. Getting to see a prisoner who had been convicted of murder was one of the more difficult challenges I had faced. Danny was a former British paratrooper who had served in Afghanistan. He had found mass graves and had been involved in many battles with the Taliban. He came to Iraq to work with a prominent security group. Intensely patriotic, Danny was from a Catholic background, and had served many years in the British Army. With the help of some of my very senior Iraqi government friends, I managed to find out which maximum security prison he was being held in.

Danny had been found guilty of murdering two fellow security guards after a whisky-fuelled argument. It was amazing to me that he did not receive the death sentence, but he was sentenced to life imprisonment in one of the most high-security Iraqi prisons. All my attempts to get to visit him via the normal diplomatic channels had totally failed, and in the end I only managed to do so by going directly to the Iraqi Prime Minister. After gaining his authorization, I eventually made the long and complicated journey to the supposedly secret location. No map or directions had been given to me, and it was a very tedious and time-consuming process. I was obliged to make phone call after phone call, and each call would tell me where to go next. Eventually I came to what was clearly a very secure area, and on reaching it I had no doubts whatsoever that I was in prison.

After many more phone calls between the Prime Minister's office and the prison governor, I eventually got to see Danny. Despite the terrible crimes that this man had committed and the facts regarding his violent past, meeting him was an amazing experience. A profound sense of love that was not my own, and compassion that was not my own, welled up from the depths of my heart.

Danny and I became immediate friends, once he had made sure that I was a real Church of England priest and that the Queen was indeed the head of our Church!

I visited him every week. I always took him a box of delicious Iraqi Abu Afif chocolates and we prayed and read the Bible together. Eventually we journeyed together through the Alpha Course. To take Danny on this journey was a deeply moving experience, and the passage that really inspired us was in the apostle John's declaration that the light shines in the darkness, and the darkness has not overcome it (John 1.5).

We knew that despite his circumstances, the light of Christ had radically overcome all darkness in Danny's life, and God's mercy, grace and forgiveness brought with them the light of life. Danny came to a full living faith in Jesus, and I baptized him in the prison governor's office. It was a truly wonderful day when Danny truly repented of his past and turned to Christ, one of the most radical and deeply moving conversions that I have ever witnessed, marked with profound remorse, wholehearted repentance and a sincere hunger to know God and be renewed. My visits continued every week, and I even took a few of our senior visitors with me to see Danny in prison, such as Lord Hylton, a senior member of the House of Lords. On Remembrance Sunday we went through the full service with him, and he stood and sang the British national anthem in order to honour our Queen and everything that she represents, including her faith in the Almighty.

As I think back to those good times with Danny, what I remember most is the true Light in the midst of such darkness, the light that shone within the prison cell, and the light that emanated from his eyes and from his soul as he moved into a place of being totally at peace with God, able to see beyond the dark shadows of his past and present reality.

We continue to hope and pray that Danny can be transferred to a British prison where the conditions are less unbearable than they are in Iraq, and we pray that in his great mercy God will give him the continued assurance of his forgiveness and his presence.

When I ponder on Danny's life, that well-known verse from the hymn 'To God Be the Glory' comes straight to my mind:

O perfect redemption, the purchase of blood,
To every believer the promise of God;
The vilest offender who truly believes,
That moment from Jesus a pardon receives.
(Lyrics by Fanny Jane Crosby, 1820–1915)

Prison ministry has been and continues to be an integral part of my work. For many, it may feel a daunting prospect and in many ways it is. What I have learned, however, is the great overwhelming force of love that does not simply compel one to visit the darkest of locations, but also enables one to touch the darkest places of a person's heart. We must always be aware of the fact that we are the hands and feet of Jesus, that we ourselves carry the mercy and the message of the Redeemer to a broken world.

Prayer

Heavenly Father, we pray for your grace, peace and comfort to be with all those individuals and families who have been victims of crime. Thank you for your outrageous forgiveness and redemption for all those who truly repent from their sins and turn to you. Let us always be mindful of the magnitude of your love and grace, and let us always be willing to share it with others, regardless of their past. Amen.

25

I lift up my eyes . . .

I lift up my eyes to the mountains –
where does my help come from?
My help comes from the LORD,
the Maker of heaven and earth.
(Psalm 121.1-2)

Three times a year, in the time of Jesus, it was essential for all practising Jews to go to Jerusalem for Passover (Pesach), Pentecost (Shavuot) and Tabernacles (Sukkot). When travelling there, it was commonplace to sing the Songs of Ascent, the psalms set aside for going up to Jerusalem. Psalm 121 was one of these. It is also a particularly popular scripture to have read at funerals today. I have often been asked to speak on this psalm.

I regularly have to tell people what the psalm is really about. There is often the general feeling that it means we should lift our eyes to the hills because that is where God is, while nothing could be further from the truth. Jerusalem is surrounded by what is described in Scripture as mountains. They are not mountains really; they are more like small hills, such as the Mount of Olives and Mount Herzog. However, despite their size, they have great biblical significance.

Traditionally, it was in these hills that a lot of the pagans had their places of worship and sacrifice, and it was to these 'high places', beset with idols, that people would lift their eyes in adoration and worship. What this psalm is saying, therefore, is: do *not* look to these hills in adoration and worship, as the pagans do. Your help comes from your Lord, your creator and maker, not from the useless pagan gods who have their shrines on the hills around Jerusalem.

Your help comes from the Lord God, the Creator of all, the one who made heaven and earth.

So as we sit down, desperately looking for the help of the Lord, let us not expect to find it in the beauty of creation, though at times we may be ministered to by the glory of nature. In reality, it is when we meditate on the maker of creation that we are truly drawn to the majesty, enormity and holiness of the Godhead.

This was almost certainly a psalm composed by David, who had spent so much of his life in the hills of Judea during his journey from shepherd boy to king. He had hidden in the hills to save his life; he was acquainted with hiding places and clefts in the rock. David knew the hills as a place of divine encounter, shelter and victory. His shepherding days, spent protecting his flock from lions and bears, trained him for what was to come. He would have been attuned to every sound of nature, as he himself made music to the Lord. Thus the hills were indeed a place of help through divine encounter and solitude with God, but they were not the *source* of help.

Whatever our situation or location, we must lift our eyes to heaven, as Jesus did when he was raising Lazarus from the tomb. We must set our mind on things above in order to adjust our view and see things from heaven's perspective. In the same way that Jesus met and communed with his Father on the mountaintops, we must reach into that higher place, through praise and worship, even if we are in the valley.

This psalm is full of the phrases of 'looking up' and 'going up', for it is indeed a psalm of ascent, one of the psalms that would be sung as the people ascended to the Temple to meet with and worship the Almighty, surrounded by the hills where the tabernacle had once stood. Today this psalm is a vital part of both the Jewish and Christian liturgical psalter. So in the same way, when we lift our eyes and fix our minds on the Almighty, we elevate ourselves; we ascend to a new dimension, a place of spiritual illumination and hope.

These psalms of ascent are also filled with terms such as 'dwelling place', which is the place of abiding in the Lord's presence and looking to him.

Central to this whole psalm is the fundamental caring nature of God. He is acutely aware of the nature of the people's pilgrimage. Despite the great difficulty posed by the journey, there is the over-riding assurance of God's provision and protection. His will is for us all to travel from glory to glory.

The Lord's caring nature is a fact that I have always been acutely aware of, physically in my life and in the multiple dangerous journeys I have made. Our Lord has always protected me. I have shown elsewhere in this book how there were times when people were not protected, but I thank God that time and time again I have been. Fundamental to this experience is the call and continual commitment to keep worshipping our Lord despite the danger we may be faced with. I have learned what it is to lift up my eyes in worship to the Lord. Despite the horrific violence that we have seen as a congregation, before the throne of grace we have been able to access help, hope, peace and joy in time of great need and suffering.

I always taught those around me to fix their gaze on a higher reality, to fix their gaze on Jesus, the King of Glory, who made a way for us to come. Others around us, whether physically or metaphorically, may have lifted up their eyes to worship at the pagan shrines in the hills, but the great call is to be like David, whose worshipful lifestyle always enabled him to see beyond. There will always be things that try to steal our gaze – hardships and hindrances that try to blur our vision and distort our perspective regarding the Lord's nature and prevent us seeing the true and living God – but we fix our eyes on him by continuing to worship him, come what may.

Of great importance in Orthodox Judaism is the role of the *shomer*, a custodian or guardian. It is not easy to translate the word precisely: you have to see it in the context of how the word is used. One very popular use is in the phrase *shomer Shabbat*, meaning a person who strives to adhere to all the rules associated with the Sabbath. The primary role of a *shomer* is to act as a legal guardian, and to many Jews this psalm reveals God as a *shomer* who watches over his promises. He is more than our protector; he is our very guardian. His eye of mercy and grace is ever upon us, and he does not slumber or sleep.

Reach out to him today, regardless of the situation you may be in and however insurmountable the problems surrounding you may appear to be. Call on his name, let your voice be heard, fix your gaze on your creator and helper, and allow his presence to lift you above your circumstance.

Prayer

Lord God, how majestic is your name! When we look up to the mountains we see you, our creator, our maker, the ruler of all the earth. You are here for us. You, our God and creator, are here - our guardian, keeper and protector. Amen.

26

He will protect you

No harm will overtake you,
no disaster will come near your tent.
For he will command his angels concerning you
to guard you in all your ways.
(Psalm 91.10-11)

Every day, thousands of people follow my public posts, and it seems that at least one person prays each day that I will come under the spiritual covering of Psalm 91. It indeed is a prayer for protection in times of great opposition and danger. The kind of danger I face may be different from what most people experience, but we all face opposition in our lives, and to all of us God gives his message of the assurance of his protection and his presence with us.

This is not an insurance package, however. It is the assurance of God's everlasting presence with us. During my student days at Cambridge I recall being told that 'prayer is not magic' - and Psalm 91 is not magic either. Sadly, there are those who approach it as if it were. So many of our loved, God-fearing people have been harmed and even killed, and yet our Lord has still cared for and been present with them and suffered with them.

So there is certainty that time and time again God will supernaturally defend and protect us, but there are also times when he will just suffer with us. There will be times when he sees the grave attacks against us, and he simply comes and stands with us and holds us and says, 'I will always love you and care for you.' Yes, there are miraculous times when our Lord will protect us and restore us, but it may not always be the case that we will survive on this earth!

I am very much aware, as I have said so many times, that 'the Lord is here, and his Spirit is with me'. What Psalm 91 means to me is that I seriously do not worry. What it means to me is that God's protection is eternal and everlasting. Like a little chick, we can shelter under the mother hen's wing and be sheltered and protected by the Almighty. We all face hard times and difficulties, but our Lord is always there, protecting and sustaining.

The thirtieth of September 2016 was a very big day in Israel, because it was the occasion of the funeral of President Shimon Peres. The leaders of the world had gathered: prime ministers and presidents, many dignitaries. Among them all sat Britain's Prince Charles.

So over 50 world leaders just happened to be staying next door to the apartment where I lived, and Israel became one major security operation. All the time I was thinking of Psalm 91: 'No harm will come near your tent.' There were tents all around the major hotels, and the security teams would not let anybody, even us, get near them. This added, I felt, a totally different meaning to this scripture, that even in the midst of heavy security, God will be with us. It is difficult to know that one's safety and protection is under the shadow of his wing, when one is surrounded by people with guns pointing in every direction.

It was a very moving experience to see the great and the good mourning the loss of this outstanding man who had come from the eastern European ghettos to be one of the leading peacemakers of the world. Lord Carey, my great mentor in life and the former Archbishop of Canterbury, wrote a poignant article about the peacemaking work we had all done together. It was under the direction of Shimon Peres that we had brought together for the first time the religious leaders from the Jewish, Christian and Muslim communities, and produced the Alexandria Declaration. To this day it is seen as the very foundation of interreligious peacemaking, not just here in Jerusalem, but throughout the world.

At the end of the day, when all the videos were looked at, we saw an incredible picture of Israeli Prime Minister Netanyahu and Abu Mazen, the President of the Palestinian National Authority, shaking hands for the first time in years. It was not just a passing handshake; it was a real encounter and an acknowledgement by the two men of a genuine relationship between them.

Yes, God will continue to protect us and enable us, despite much opposition. Recently I celebrated the twenty-sixth anniversary of my ordination. I had had no idea then what lay ahead, no idea what a strange and international ministry I would have. But the Lord knew.

Prayer

O Lord our God, we give you thanks that even though prayer is not magic, you are always there with us. We give you thanks that we always gain protection under the shadow of your wing. We give you thanks that we move powerfully with you, our strength and our protector.

Thank you, Lord, that you are always with us. Amen.

27

Forgiveness

If we confess our sins, he is faithful and just and will forgive us
our sins and purify us from all unrighteousness.
(1 John 1.9)

Today as I write, we are in the second day of Rosh HaShanah,
the Jewish Feast of the New Year. Most things are silent, as today
is a *yom tov*[1] – a day like the Sabbath, when shops are shut, people
don't travel, and so on. This day is seen as a time of repentance,
mourning *and* celebration. It is the point of entry into the ten 'Days
of Awe', the period of repentance leading to the awesome day of
Yom Kippur, the Day of Atonement. In the period of the Temple,
sheep would be slaughtered on that day by the high priest on the
altar. Without an active temple, this no longer happens.

As Christians, we believe that Jesus was the final sacrifice and
provided for us himself as the perfect atoning sacrifice. We are often
separated from one another, yet are committed to working together
for reconciliation.

Early today, while it was still dark, tens of thousands of people
descended on the whole plaza around the Western Wall in
Jerusalem, singing and praying in repentance, taking part in the
act of Selichot, the penitential prayers of Rosh HaShanah. It was one
of the most incredible religious experiences I have ever witnessed.
Selichot comes from the Hebrew word *selichah*, which means
'forgiveness'. If you look up Selichot online, you will be able to see
the ceremony, which takes place at the Western Wall.

---

1 Hebrew for 'good day'.

For Christian Iraqis, the biggest fast of the year is the fast of Jonah, during which believers fast from food and water for three whole days and nights, the main focus being repentance and returning to God. Nineveh, the city to which Jonah was sent to preach, is located north of Baghdad, just before Iraq turns into Kurdistan. To this day Nineveh is the only city that is predominantly Christian in Iraq. Sadly, the shrine of Jonah was completely destroyed by ISIS, but Iraqi Christians see him and his obedience as a major part of their heritage.

For traditional Western Christians, the great time of repentance and fasting is what has become known to us as Lent, the 40 days leading up to Easter, the Feast of Resurrection. This is very different in nature, but also a moving time of great repentance.

I will never forget the time I first entered Coventry Cathedral. It was the season of Lent, and the day before I was to be interviewed for the job that would set my ministry firmly upon the path of forgiveness and reconciliation. As I walked into the cathedral, the choir was processing, singing the words 'Lord, have mercy.' It was very different from what happens at the Western Wall during Selichot, yet in a strange way very similar. In both cases there is an honest yearning to move closer to God in forgiveness and repentance. Christians rejoice in the assurance that the Holy One of Israel is the only one who can take away all our sins and cleanse us from all unrighteousness.

Coventry Cathedral has at its very heart the ministry of forgiveness and reconciliation. On the wall of the ruined sanctuary there, you can find these two words: 'Father Forgive'. I wrote a book with that title, which explains in full how those words came to be there, following the bombing of the cathedral on 14 November 1940, during the Second World War.

As we continue to struggle to work for reconciliation, those words remain in our hearts. Forgiveness is the core of the Christian faith. It is an element in Judaism, but not in the same way as it is in Christianity, where it is the very heart of salvation. God in Christ has forgiven us, so we in Christ forgive others.

One of the joys of writing about forgiveness on the 'day of awe' here in Israel is in learning about the Jewish concept of forgiveness. I have learned that Rosh HaShanah is very much about us forgiving one another. So the children in Orthodox families go around saying sorry to their brothers and sisters and asking their friends to forgive them. Would it not be good if we could have a forgiveness day like that, when we too could walk around sharing forgiveness? In doing so, we too would find forgiveness and wholeness. In our daily family life we are surrounded by brokenness and pain, often caused by unforgiveness. Forgiveness is about healing, restoration and reconciliation. Let's live forgiveness.

Prayer

Lord, help me to forgive, especially those who have hurt those I love. Teach me the true power of your cross. Amen.

28
Arise

A righteous man falls seven times, and rises again.
(Proverbs 24.16 RSV)

We all make mistakes. We all fall down and cry, 'No, never again!'
One of my favourite quotes comes from a star of the silent screen, Mary Pickford: 'It is not falling that is so bad; it is not getting up.' We will all fall, and King Solomon reminds us in Proverbs 24.16 that though the righteous person may fall seven times, he or she will arise. Each time we fall we learn a new lesson, and each time we arise we are a new person. Each time, the Lord is saying again and again, 'Do not fear: I am near.'

We are all faced with the need to make changes, but this is never easy. As the great Rabbi Moshe ben Maimon observes in his work, *The Guide for the Perplexed*: 'A sudden transition from one opposite to another is impossible and therefore man, according to his nature, is not capable of abandoning suddenly all to which he was accustomed.'[1] Making major changes in our lives is certainly possible, and while as Christians we believe that transformation takes place as soon as a sinner repents and believes, it is worth being mindful of this observation so that certain changes can be made slowly and one step at a time. In this sense, process and progress can be experienced in a positive and uplifting way.

As I continue to struggle with ill health, I remain fully aware that he who has called me will not fail me. I have been weak, and on several occasions have literally fallen because of my poor sense of balance, but God has always set me back on my feet and given me

---

1   Rabbi Moshe ben Maimon, *Guide for the Perplexed* (c.1190), 3.23.

the strength to go on. I continue to believe that he is my healer and that the best is yet to come.

This strength to arise comes from the fact that in my weakness he is strong and from my constant awareness that I am wearing the armour of God. When my body is weak, my spirit and soul are strong and protected.

Most of the pictures of me, those that appear in places where I speak, include photos of me in my military body armour, which I used to have to wear in Baghdad. When I speak to children in church, I often take the body armour with me. I used to get them to try it out and punch me with their fists. Of course this never hurt me but did hurt the aggressor (to such an extent that I now let them test it with my walking stick). This is a great analogy of what happens in the spiritual realm when we are wearing the armour that God has given us. The attacker soon gives up because his strength is weakened and he himself is damaged. The more he attacks the armour and finds that it is impenetrable, the more he flees from the scene. For me personally, I believe that often it was this heavenly armour, combined with divine instruction and angelic assistance, that protected me more than the bulletproof vests that I wore. Remaining clothed in the armour that the apostle Paul exhorts us to clothe ourselves in has enabled me to stay in a place where my spiritual discernment and intuition have been sharp, my ability to hear God's voice strong, and my awareness of his presence constant. Here is Paul's famous description of the believer's armour from Ephesians 6.10–17:

Finally, be strong in the Lord and in his mighty power. Put on the full armour of God, so that you can take your stand against the devil's schemes. For our struggle is not against flesh and blood, but against the rulers, against the authorities, against the powers of this dark world and against the spiritual forces of evil in the heavenly realms. Therefore put on the full armour of God, so that when the day of evil comes, you may be able to stand your ground, and after you have done everything, to stand. Stand firm then, with the belt of truth buckled round your waist, with the breastplate of righteousness in place, and with your feet fitted with the readiness that comes from the gospel of peace. In addition to all this, take up the shield of faith, with which you can extinguish all the flaming arrows of the evil one. Take the helmet of salvation and the sword of the Spirit, which is the word of God.

I see too many unarmed, or partially armed, Christians walking around unable to deal with life and unaware that to become a disciple of Jesus is to be part of an 'army'. The Scriptures are overflowing with references to this. The Church needs to reflect on what it really means to be armed with the full armour of God and to overcome 'by the word of our testimony and the blood of the Lamb'.[2] We need to remain aware, especially in places like the Middle East, that our struggle is with spiritual forces and principalities, which means that one should not even consider pursuing ministry there when unarmed or only partially armed. The same was the case with the church Paul was addressing in Ephesus. Each part of the armour is crucial and all the components complement one another. The power that comes through wielding the sword of the Spirit, the unshakeable word of God, can only be at its height if the other defensive pieces of armour are being properly worn.

Whatever our profession and location may be, we, as Christians, must know that it is a dangerous thing to be unarmed. The wonderful reality is that, unlike military armour, which is heavy, weighty and cumbersome (those I show it to often have trouble lifting it), the spiritual armour that comes from above is light and weightless, not subject to gravity. We can leap and soar in this weightless armour, and it is more dazzling than any armour known in the history of the world, because it is all about Jesus, whose burden is light. This armour is also 'light' in the other sense of that word: 'The night is far spent, the day is at hand: let us therefore cast off the works of darkness, and let us put on the armour of light' (Romans 13.12 KJV).

---

2   See Revelation 12.11.

Being fully armed does not simply bring self-illumination and enlightenment in terms of our true identity in Christ. It also enables us to emanate a supernatural light that shines forth in the darkest of places. This, as we know, is at the very heart of the great commission to dispel darkness and of the great call to 'arise and shine, for our light has come'.[3]

We must thus arise and be strong; we must put on our armour and be radiant. Arise and shine, you weary ones, and walk on in the armour of his light.

Prayer

Lord God, we thank you that you have not left us unresourced, unequipped or unarmed. We thank you for the perfect armour that you have created for us, and we ask that we may live in the reality of being always prepared and ready for battle.

Help us all to be overcomers and to walk closely with you, so that we may be enforcers of the great victory over death and darkness that you have already achieved. Amen.

---

3 See Isaiah 60.1.

29

Perfect love casts out fear

There is no fear in love. But perfect love drives out fear, because fear has to do with punishment. The one who fears is not made perfect in love.
(1 John 4.18)

As I write, I am on a plane on my way to Israel, the place I love and know. I was there just three days ago and yet I am still excited to be going back. So much of my life has been spent in places of great tension and violence. Yet I have never had any fear. Maybe today you are living with great anxiety and fear. Everything seems so terrible and there seems no way out. Where shall I go? What shall I do? You may face despair and hopelessness; but then remember, there is love. Human love always causes pain. Love hurts. When we are in love, we always know pain. What have we done and said to the other? Why is he or she doing this to us? The pain can be so great when someone we love turns away from us.

But real love casts out fear, including the fear of pain. When people ask me how I manage to keep going and not fear when I am working in such dangerous situations, I always say it is through the perfect love that drives out fear. I always used to say it was through the love of the children, but my colleagues reminded me that it is not just the children who love me: there are many others as well who are a major source of inspiration.

Yet when I look seriously at my work across the Middle East, it is above all the children who have loved and inspired me. This is also true in the UK and USA. In Israel-Palestine, Jordan and Iraq I have found the running of schools to be a major part of my life. I have no teacher training or experience, and yet I find myself the president of schools in four different continents.

Several of the children in these schools are like my unofficial adopted children. I now have many godchildren too. At the last count there were 33 godchildren, and more in waiting. I always said I would never have more than 20 godchildren, then it was 30, and the number is still growing. Most of these children I actually baptized or dedicated myself. All of them are very special to me and all of them I truly love.

It is funny when you find yourself conducting the weddings of your godchildren and eventually baptizing their children. The only reason I can do my work, which is often daunting, is because of the inspiration I receive from them.

I have often been surrounded with this love. Perfect love truly does remove fear. It is a love that metaphorically sets your heart on fire – and that fire destroys all fear. This love is like a refiner's fire that purifies gold: it removes that which is impure and leaves only that which is pure and holy. It is the fire of refinement, not destruction; it is the purifying love of God's purity, which only comes from this true refinement.

Nowadays there is rightly more concern than ever about the protection of children. There is often a lot of frustration about the continual Criminal Records Bureau (CRB) procedures that people always have to go through now if they are to have any connection with children through their work – a frustration sometimes voiced among the clergy, where sadly there is a history of inappropriate behaviour by some of them towards young people. I fully support the CRB requirements. When I talk about the importance of children's love in my work and ministry, I make clear that all our work with children has to be undertaken within clear rules and regulations.

We will not get to heaven without pain. As Romans 8.13 states: 'If you live according to the flesh, you will die; but if by the Spirit you put to death the misdeeds of the body, you will live.' The kind of love that I am talking about, which casts out all fear, is intrinsically linked to the refiner's fire. It will drive us through the fire, leaving us free of fear, burning instead with love for God, and for those around us – including for the children, and indeed for ourselves.

We must never underestimate the significance of children in our Lord's ministry. People often look at ministries like mine, working flat out in the middle of war zones, and say: well, children could never be involved in them. On the contrary: without those little children I would not have been able to do my work. Their presence is at the root of that perfect love that drives out all fear; that has enabled me not to take care, but to take risks. Risks for his kingdom, risks for his glory, risks for the healing of the nations. Risks in seeing and knowing that it is perfect love that removes all fear.

Prayer

Heavenly Father, we thank you for your perfect love. We thank you that it removes all fear. We thank you for how you so often use little children as the source of this Love.

Lord, may your love continue to lift all fear from our lives, so that we may take risks for you. We love you so much, Lord. Amen.

30

Sheep and goats

When the Son of Man comes in his glory, and all the angels
with him, he will sit on his glorious throne. All the nations will
be gathered before him, and he will separate the people one
from another as a shepherd separates the sheep from the goats.
He will put the sheep on his right and the goats on his left.
(Matthew 25.31–33)

In the rural, semi-rural and desert parts of the Middle East, you
are continually faced with sheep and goats. For people not familiar
with the territory, they look somewhat similar. The quick way of
telling the difference is to look at the tails. Sheep's tails go down,
and as a rule goats' tails go up. They look superficially the same, but
they are different.

In this passage from Matthew Jesus is talking about the last day,
when he will return, the final 'day of judgement'. He can see all the
people and they all look much the same. In the Middle East the sheep
and the goats are similar. He does not say you can identify them by
their tails. He says it's not a matter of what they look like, but what
they actually do. You see, according to our Lord's simile in Matthew
25.31–46, the sheep live in love and the goats do not.

What is living in love? It is feeding the hungry, and giving a
drink to those who are thirsty; giving clothes to those who have no
clothes, giving homes to the homeless, going to visit those held in
prison and treating the sick.

There is such joy in serving our Lord and Master. That is what
we have sought to do in our ministry, serving the persecuted
Church. These people are our family. They are not just the distant persecuted Church; they are your brothers and sisters and

children. They need food, clothes and healthcare. They need love and education. They need more than we could ever imagine. How is all this done? Through you. You might not be the one on the ground doing the work, but I am, and I can only do this if you are with me and enable me. In the natural state of things, I should not be able to do this. I am ill with MS. I have a far from perfect body. I am mainly confined to a wheelchair, unable to walk more than a few steps. The great news is that God always enables us to do what he calls us to do.

Behind our ministry lies the story of the glory of God, which sums up the total of who I am and what I do. The glory of God is what my faith, my work and my calling are all about. It is a ministry of word, spirit *and* action. I know of no more suitable passage for this than Jesus' parable about the sheep and the goats. The sum total of the gospel is not just about words but also action. Ministry is not just about what you say and believe; it is about what you do.

The whole focus of the charity I run, Jerusalem MERIT, is about putting into action the redemptive work of transformation. It is not enough just to *say* that we are doing the right things; we have to be physically *doing* them. I always say we have to be both praying and paying for peace. When we pray, we should seek to truly understand what things we need to pray for. We need a full understanding of the political, social, economic and spiritual dimensions aiding the conflict. We need to pray about difficult individuals whom God needs to radically change, and to be persistent in praying for the needed change.

When it comes to paying for peace, we need to once again be specific about the needs we have to pay for, what we pay for and how we do it. In my work and ministry we clearly divide these issues into five particular areas:

1 The provision of basic relief – food, drink and clothing.
2 The provision of housing and suitable accommodation.
3 The provision of proper healthcare and medication. In all the areas we have worked, we have also provided full medical and dental clinics.

4 The provision of education for children. The schools we run provide a comprehensive education for children aged from 4 to 18, giving the foundation for training and developing the peacemakers of the future.

5 The area of reconciliation – one of the largest and most complicated areas. Peacemaking may sound nice, good and easy, but it can be complex and expensive. It often involves long journeys to countries considered safe for representatives of warring parties to meet in; they also often demand exactly the right kind of accommodation and food.

I had to learn about the last point the hard way: by making a lot of mistakes. Early on, I set up an international meeting of religious leaders from Iraq in England and America. I had assumed originally that these were people of faith, and therefore that they would appreciate the simplicity of a monastic guest house with good private rooms. I was severely mistaken, and they all refused to stay in the residence for even one day. I realized very early on that you could not provide such leaders with anything except the highest-quality hotel accommodation. This has sadly been an issue we have had to bear in mind throughout our work. Peacemaking is usually highly complex. When it works, and it often has worked, it saves many lives and lots of money, but once again you have to take risks to make it happen. We had to realize that even though we want to do things simply and cheaply, sometimes we just cannot for the greater cause of God's kingdom. To me, the real 'sheep' are the ones who, whatever they look like, really want to do the work of a peacemaker and bring about healing, wholeness and reconciliation. We are all called to do this.

Prayer

Show me your way, Lord, show me the way. Give me the wisdom to know the sheep from the goats. Help me love, so that I may bring unity; and enable me to maintain a level of simplicity.

Lord, help there to be unity among the sheep so that we can do the work of a peacemaker and bring about healing, wholeness and reconciliation. Amen.

31
From Baghdad to Jerusalem

And my God will meet all your needs according to the riches
of his glory in Christ Jesus.
(Philippians 4.19)

I loved my life in Baghdad: it was my home. I loved the people,
the food, the River Tigris, the ayatollahs and the worship.

Then the terrible day came when my friend Justin Welby, the
Archbishop of Canterbury, told me I had to leave. He rightly
pointed out that I could do more alive than dead. So I went back to
Jerusalem and Jordan. It truly was a supernatural journey, and my
life has never been the same since.

Despite being based away from Baghdad, I have returned for
short visits, supposedly secret so that the bad guys who had set a
price on my head did not know I was there. Jerusalem was where my
Middle East life and work began, and I had never wanted to leave
Jerusalem and cross the River Jordan, but when I did so, I never
really wished to return. I had seen so much of the glory of God in
the terrible context of Baghdad that I did not want to leave.

When I finally did leave Iraq, a great deal happened and it was
as if the glory I had known in Baghdad had returned to the land
of the Holy One. I loved being back. I started to see countless
glorious things happening there just as I had seen in Baghdad.
I was happy in Israel. I realized yet again that, whenever you are
where God wants you to be, he will give you joy. He certainly did
this for me.

While my stem cell treatment was still working, there was reason
to go to Erbil in northern Iraq-Kurdistan, the place I often refer to
as 'pretend Iraq'. Erbil and Dohuk are very interesting historic cities

but are located in a land that has a different government from Iraq. Kurdistan has its own separate flag and language.

As I write today, I am in the real Iraq and its capital, Baghdad. It is like being home and I love it. Despite not being back at St George's Church, many people from there are visiting me.

The problems in Baghdad remain very considerable. Daesh (or ISIS) has had a profound effect. The above passage from Philippians is a key one, concerning God's reassurance and provision for his people. Throughout my week in Iraq I have been continually presented with different needs. Every day countless numbers of people come, showing me great love. Most ask for assistance, but many who really need help do not even ask, and those are the people I am especially drawn to. I have heard the stories countless times, and they are all real, but the provision is so small. I returned to England still missing my people in Iraq, aware more than ever of the needs I have to try to meet.

My verse for the week was certainly Philippians 4.19: 'And my God will meet all your needs according to the riches of his glory in Christ Jesus.'

We all have huge needs all the time. It grieves me when I cannot help the most needy. However, we have to learn that all we require comes from the Almighty. I am aware that God has often used me as the channel. The downside is that in many circles there is the belief that I am very rich, ignoring the reality that I live by faith and often do not even have a salary. When people have a need and ask what to do, many times the answer is, 'Go to Abouna Andrew.' And many times I thank God that he does enable me to provide. So often, I just sit down and say, 'Help me, Lord.' I have nothing and he always does help.

It is usually when you've exhausted your resources that you truly trust. During my most recent trip to Baghdad, I had my regular stem cell treatment for my MS. Usually I experience a rapid and radical improvement. This time I did not. It is very hard for me, realizing that I cannot even walk more than a few steps any more, and have to do everything from a wheelchair. As usual, I am surrounded by so many triumphant Christians saying, 'If only you believed properly, you would be healed.' Well, I do believe properly, and I am not.

This takes me back to the fact that there are many people who are very ill, yet still have so much faith that the Lord can touch them. They are still struggling and still waiting. I find myself continually called to serve these dear people, those who have great needs and have not yet received great answers. It is to these people that my Lord so often speaks and simply says, 'I am still with you. I will not leave you. I will provide what you really need, which is me.'

When you realize that you have nothing, you realize that he is everything. When you know that he is everything, you realize that he is indeed what his Hebrew name, beginning with Y or J, actually means: 'the one who is and was and is to come'. The one who holds past, present and future.

In Hebrew, wonderfully, the name of God is HaShem, which simply means 'the Name'. For the name of the Almighty is indeed above every other name. This is a term that is understood among many Christians, because it is so often applied to Jesus.

There is a very popular song written by a young New Zealand woman, Naida Hearn, in 1974. She was overwhelmed by the different names applied to Jesus. So she wrote these amazing words. To me, sitting here in Jerusalem, her song applies to 'the Name':

Jesus, name above all names
Beautiful Saviour, glorious Lord.
Emmanuel, God is with us
Blessed Redeemer, Living word.

He does indeed provide all our needs because he is the Name above every other name. He is simply HaShem – the Name.

Faced with this truth, all we can do is praise him: 'Lord God, we praise you that you are the Name above all names, the name that provides all our needs according to his riches in glory. We know that our Lord is indeed always with us.'

During and following my trip to Baghdad, I had to come to terms with the terrible fact that the stem cell treatment was no longer working. The treatment had really been like a supernatural gift of God, and had kept me going for several years. My neurologist in England was clear that he did not think it would work any longer. The last four times I had the treatment, it failed. I had to realize that now my only hope was the supernatural power of our Lord. Despite all these problems, I knew that my work could not finish or stop. So I have persevered, and by God's grace the work has continued to go very well.

What I find very strange is that, even with my physical problems, God has used me increasingly in the ministry of healing. There are so many people saying that I have not been healed because I do not truly believe. Well, I do believe, trust, and know that God can and will heal me. In the past few months a major part of my ministry has been spent with people who have been severely hurt by people holding them responsible for their lack of healing. To them, God has had me say, 'Do not fear. I am still near you and with you.'

Prayer

Thank you, Lord, for being our everything, our healer, protector and Saviour. We thank you that you never leave us, always stay with us and always love us. Amen.

32
In and out

The LORD will guard your going out and your coming in
From this time forth and forever.
(Psalm 121.8 NASB)

I have been very blessed in the last few weeks to have a wonderful young man interning with me, called Patrick Owen. His family are good friends of ours and I officiated at his parents' wedding. After he had travelled with me to Baghdad, Jerusalem and Amman in Jordan, I asked him what really stood out to him from his three-nation trip and he said something really interesting. He replied, 'In Baghdad and Jordan, everybody wants to get out, but in Israel, everybody wants to get in.'

It dawned on me that this was absolutely true. We are continually meeting people who want to get to Israel. There are those who want to prove that they are Jewish so they can 'make *aliya*', which is the official name for the right of return to Israel. Then there are so many people who feel they are being called by God to minister in Israel. I am sure some people actually are . . .

But why? I am drawn to one of the psalms of ascent that was used in worship as people journeyed up to Jerusalem in order to sacrifice to God in the Temple. The passage above assures us that the Lord is there, when we go out and come in. This does not mean that everything is guaranteed to be good: it is not. As I write, today is Yom HaShoah, the Israeli Holocaust Memorial Day. This day commemorates one of the biggest tragedies in history, when six million Jews were killed, along with many others.

In the wake of the Nazi tragedy, the modern state of Israel was born. The soil, nation and hope of the promised land came alive again. This land which so many Jews and others want to enter. This land which is partially seen as the fulfilment of messianic hope. To both Christians and Jews, the birth of the state of Israel leads one to believe in partial messianic fulfilment. Everybody wants to come into Israel because it is a land of messianic hope; it is the land that looks forward to the coming of the Messiah – for the first or second time, depending on one's theological understanding.

While the land of Israel is where everybody is pleased to be, just next door, in Palestinian areas, and in Jordan and Iraq, there are people who do not want to be there. These refugees are just waiting to move on. Most of those we work with in Jordan are Iraqis seeking asylum overseas. Most have been waiting years, roughly since the time of the great exodus in 2014, when ISIS began its terrorist activity in Iraq and people started to flee for their lives.

Most of us do not live in this state of uncertainty, yet we often live with unknowing and insecurity. We feel perhaps that we are going in and out of our relationship with the Almighty. The one thing I have learned for sure from our refugees is the assurance that we have not lost the presence of our Lord. They may have lost everything, in material terms, but our community never loses the assurance that the Lord is here and his Spirit is with us.

As I have said so often, one thing I can never deny is the response of my adopted daughter Lina in Baghdad many years ago. When asked, among the bombs, why she was happy, she said, 'When you have lost everything, Jesus is all you have left.'

Our Lord is the one who helps us. He is the supernatural and the real, and even when we seem to have nothing, he is everything. This is the song of ascent. We may not physically be going up to the Temple to pray and sacrifice, but we are going on our way to the heavenly kingdom of the Almighty. We are all on our way into the presence of the Almighty and finally out into the heavenly kingdom.

Prayer

Lord, we ask questions: 'Where are you, Lord, where?' You always reply, 'I am near and beside you.' You help us on the way.

Help us when we do not know where we are going. Show us the way, because you indeed are the Way, the Truth and the Life. Thank you that you never leave us. Amen.

33
Finding refuge

Give us counsel and make a decision. Shelter us at noonday
with shade that is as dark as night. Hide the refugees; do not
betray the one who flees.
(Isaiah 16.3 HCSB)

I have always been moved by the plight of refugees and inter-
ested in the existence of cities of refuge as we see them in Scripture.
It is interesting to consider that Jesus himself was a refugee: his
parents knew what it was to have no home and to be forced out of
their native land due to danger. From the time of Abraham, right
through the generations, the notions of homelessness, of being a
foreigner, seeking asylum and refuge in another land, are present
throughout Scripture. Likewise, the teachings within the Torah
concerning the welcoming of the foreigner – and the teachings of
Jesus himself – are focused on our treatment of the stranger, the
outcast, the homeless one who is seeking a place of refuge.

For me, the beauty of the psalms is that God himself is seen as the
ultimate dwelling place: 'Lord, you have been our dwelling-place
throughout all generations' (Psalm 90.1). He is the only sure place of
refuge, and both of these expressions, 'dwelling place' and 'refuge',
are used continually throughout the Bible: 'I cry to you, O LORD;
I say, "You are my refuge, my portion in the land of the living"'
(Psalm 142.5 ESV).

Ultimately, God wants to enable us to think spiritually beyond
geographical or national boundaries to a place of rest and an eternal
abode that can only be found in him. This reality is continued in
the ministry and teaching of Jesus, who exhorts us to abide in him,
to make him our home: 'Abide in me, and I in you. As the branch

cannot bear fruit of itself, except it abide in the vine; no more can ye, except ye abide in me' (John 15.4 KJV).

As set out in the Torah, certain cities in Ancient Israel were selected to be cities of refuge, safe places where those in trouble could reside.[1] There were many reasons why all the cities of refuge were Levitical cities, the main ones being that these cities were specially consecrated to the Lord because it was to the priests and Levites that the people looked as administrators of justice.

The existence of these places makes me think of Jordan and its identity as a place of refuge for persecuted Christians to find a haven. My people there have no desire to return to Baghdad as it is so dark and dangerous. Their goal is to start a whole new life, and many have done so in countries such as Canada, the USA and Australia, while others continue to wait patiently for news on the status of their visa applications. Although they have no rights to welfare, education or employment in Jordan, and the United Nations continues to ignore their plight, Jordan with its benevolent dictator has become a place of refuge; more precisely, the capital Amman has become for my homeless Christian Iraqis a city of refuge.

Of course, the burden upon my heart is not just for refugees but for 'internally displaced people' (IDPs). As ISIS entered northern Iraq, the biggest crisis in history for the Iraqi Christians and Yazidis began. Both groups were seen by the terrorists as not being properly monotheistic religions. The Christians were condemned because of their belief in the Trinity – thus 'three gods' – while the Yazidis were commonly seen as being devil-worshippers. Each group underwent brutal persecution and was forced to flee. Yazidis in particular were no strangers to persecution. Under the government of Saddam Hussein, Yazidis were forced to identify themselves as Kurds, and heavy-handed tactics were used to oppress and reclassify them.

I had been talking about the Yazidis for years and regularly meeting with members of the community and their leaders well before they became a 'discussed' group. Many people in the West had

1   See, for instance, Numbers 35; Deuteronomy 4; Deuteronomy 19; Joshua 20.

never heard of them, and even in Iraq there were very few individuals who knew of their existence or their beliefs.

I would often visit the community when I was in the north of Iraq. I always went to their holy mountain of Sinjar and spent hours talking to their leaders. It was a very interesting experience trying to establish exactly who the Yazidis were, and what they believed. It became very obvious to me that there were great similarities between the Yazidis and other groups I had grown to know well, such as the Druze and the Samaritans, as well as the Mandaeans (followers of John the Baptist), many of whom were violently attacked and kidnapped in Iraq because they were goldsmiths. My heart breaks for these persecuted minorities.

During some of our significant meetings between the years 2005 and 2008, when we tried to prepare declarations against terrorist activity in Iraq, we saw a radical onslaught by ISIS against the Yazidi people and the invasion of their mountain, Mount Sinjar. The violent attacks included targeted aggression against all groups who were not seen as being real believers in monotheism, such as the Mandaeans and the Yazidis. ISIS justified its policy of attacking non-monotheistic 'pagan' groups by declaring them as 'devil-worshippers'. The attacks on Sinjar were extreme. Many of the men were killed. Many young men and boys were recruited by ISIS, forced to convert and often trained as fighters. What happened to the girls and women is difficult to describe. They were kidnapped and held as enforced sex-slaves – some being raped up to five times a day. Those taken as slaves included girls as young as five, up to women in their sixties. These women were treated desperately and cut off from one another. A few of them managed to escape and tell their stories. When the reality of this crisis became known, we tried to see what we could do to help.

We knew that under no circumstances could we ever pay money to get any of these women back and so we had no idea how we would ever succeed in helping them. We then learned that some of the ISIS terrorists were the very people we had worked with and supported when they were living under attack in the al-Anbar area of Iraq known as the Sunni Triangle. This included residents of the

Saddam heartlands, including the towns of Ramadi and Fallujah, and Saddam Hussein's home town of Tikrit. These people had all been very hurt by the process of de-Baathification: they had lost their homes, property and businesses, and had ultimately resorted to terrorism in an attempt to regain identity and power through conflict.

The very essence of my work was fulfilling the biblical injunction to set the captive free; for years it has been a vital part of my ministry. It was a huge challenge to locate the dangerous men with whom we had worked, and it was disturbing to meet those who had once been our friends but had now given themselves over to terrorism. It was without doubt one of the most distressing and frustrating endeavours of my whole ministry. When some captives were finally released – after our pleas to the kidnappers to treat us with the kindness that we had shown them – we tried to find them accommodation, often providing housing for whole Yazidi communities, both male and female. This we were able to do in the safety of Kurdistan; one such place was a very large chicken-shed compound on the outskirts of Erbil.

Being among the people who had escaped was distressing in the extreme. They were living as peasants in one of the darkest and most deprived environments I had ever witnessed. They were not classed as refugees because they were actually still in their own country. Eventually, whole camps for these horribly victimized people were established – many living simply in tents, or in military cabins, the kind that I and my colleagues had lived in after the coalition invasion. Most of these camps were segregated between Yazidis, Christians and other groups. We provided them with the basics of food, water and clothing, as they had been stripped of everything. The one positive thing that remains in my memory is the immense delight the children expressed when we gave them bags of mixed sweets. Our Christian ministry among the Yazidis has been a major long-term endeavour, and a true expression of love. It was not the focus of our efforts, but to our joy we did see a few people come to know and trust Jesus.

Many Yazidis still reside in Erbil, but they all want to return to their mountain.

Among the other minorities, the Mandaeans and Druze whom I mentioned earlier, there was a very similar experience. To this day, there are those still working seriously to try to provide therapy and psychological support for the thousands affected by this tragedy.

Prayer

Father, we thank you that, as the psalmist states, you are our dwelling place. We pray that you will enable us to reach those without a place of refuge, and bring practical help and healing to the homeless wherever we are. We pray that you will reveal yourself as the true place of security for each wounded soul. Amen.

34
And all shall be well

And we know that all things work together for good to them that love God, to them who are the called according to his purpose.
(Romans 8.28 KJV)

When I have asked people what their favourite verses were, Romans 8.28 came up again and again. Even among those of us with great faith, there is the continuous issue of living with really bad and dangerous circumstances. Yet in the midst of that darkness, when everything is awful and frightening, we need to know that our Lord is there and he will in the end ensure that everything is all right. It brings me back again to the Arabic saying, *Yom asal, yom basal*, which means, as I have mentioned before, 'honey days and onion days'. There are indeed good days and bad days; sweet days and crying days. There are days when we do not know what is happening. We hold on to the fact that we know, in the end, that God does know what is going on, and is totally in control. The fact is that in the end God will always protect and take care of his people.

Last week I was in Wales and went to teach in a high school A-level Religious Studies class. Not one of the 13 young people in the class believed in God. Some said they were atheists, but I doubted whether any of them really had enough faith not to believe in God. They asked about my work. I explained what I do, and they said, 'How do you know that the birth of Jesus really happened in Bethlehem?' I went over with them the very significant evidence that the birth of Jesus took place in Bethlehem, where I spend so much of my life.

Our faith starts with a cradle in Bethlehem and ends with a cross in Jerusalem. From cradle to grave, we go on a journey with Jesus. It is a journey of immense suffering and miracles; a story of glory, healing and provision. It's a story from having nothing to having everything; from being tempted in the wilderness to the glory of the Transfiguration. The needs are so great, yet our Lord promises that 'all things will work together for good to those who love God'.

This verse is quoted frequently by Christians to Christians when things are difficult or have gone seriously wrong. So often, people have said this to me when things have been awful. But we need to be careful how we use this verse. Just to use it like a sticking plaster on people's pain is not the answer. We need to always show people that God is the answer to their pain, but we cannot just quote a simple passage without showing that we are willing to be the hands and feet of Jesus, and to provide for people's needs.

Yes, God is our provider, but when somebody is critically ill or has just had a loved one killed or taken into captivity, he or she needs to have a deep revelation of the goodness of God that surpasses any form of rational explanation or visible evidence.

There are occasions when we can only pray, in complete honesty, 'Lord God, we know that all things do indeed work together for good when we love you. We do love you, Lord, but sometimes it just seems so hard. Why, Lord, why? When will it be good?' He just says 'Wait and see', and we respond, 'We *are* waiting, Lord.' In all these crisis situations, my response is always the same: we just have to express our immense love to God – and if this is too hard, start by saying, 'Lord, help us to love you.'

As I was preparing this meditation, there was yet another major terrorist attack, this time at a music event attended by many innocent young people in Manchester. The cry goes out again: 'Why, Lord, why?' There is never an easy answer.

These youngsters were so near the cradle, yet ended so prematurely in the grave. There is no easy answer, but there is the assurance that in the pain and suffering our Lord is also suffering. For he is also the Lord who asked 'Why?' So whatever the situation, our Lord cries with us. He shares our pain, brokenness and desperation, and takes us in his arms and loves us.

There is no writing better than John Bunyan's classic novel *Pilgrim's Progress* to help us maintain our perspective. The story concerns the pilgrim, Christian, on a journey to the promised land. His journey is our journey. It is full of trials and temptations, pain and difficulty. In the course of his travels, Christian arrives at the Palace Beautiful, which is a place of respite.

He is met there by Prudence, and she asks him the great question. In contemporary language it is, 'How do you keep going when the going gets tough?'

Prudence: Can you remember by what means you find your annoyances, at times, as if they were vanquished?

Christian: Yes, when I think of what I saw at the cross, that will do it; and when I look upon my embroidered coat, that will do it; also when I look into the roll that I carry in my bosom, that will do it; and when my thoughts wax warm about whither I am going, that will do it.[1]

In other words, what we saw at the cross will always keep us going. When we look at all that God has provided, that will sustain us. When we look at the Holy Bible, that will encourage us. When we think about where we are going, that will sustain us.

Prudence: And what is it that makes you so desirous to go to Mount Zion?

Christian: Why, there I hope to see him alive that did hang dead on the cross; and there I hope to be rid of all those things

---

1   For those unfamiliar with Bunyan's story, the 'embroidered coat' is the garment given to him at the foot of the cross, at the start of his pilgrimage (see the 'change of raiment' mentioned in Zechariah 3.4 KJV). The 'roll', with a seal upon it, was given to him at the same time and contains the Word of Truth (see Ephesians 1.13); Christian is to look at the roll as he runs.

that to this day are in me and annoyances to me; there they say there is no death.

Where we are finally going is where we will see the wonder and glory of the resurrection in all its fullness.

Prayer

Lord, we take comfort that you are here with us. You take this pain with you. You took it at the cross, and every day the pain is with you.

We may at times feel that we live in a Good Friday world, but the resurrection is coming. We thank you that joy comes in the morning. Amen.

35
Out of the tomb

But God raised him from the dead on the third day and
caused him to be seen.
(Acts 10.40)

In this chapter I first want to tell you about a man from my
Baghdad parish by the name of Wissam Benham. Wissam is
the Christian father of eight children, one of whom was killed
(see below), and the husband to a beautiful God-fearing wife.
They were successful people in Baghdad and their business was
doing well. They owned livestock and were well respected in the
community.

When ISIS terrorists forced themselves into their home, they ravaged it and burned down everything the family had. Wissam was
taken away handcuffed, and then buried alive in a hole, which
was cemented over. His wife, distraught at home, was violently
pushed to the ground as she held her baby in her arms. The baby's
head hit the floor, which led to a brain clot; within a few hours the
child was dead. Unfortunately, the scenario I have described, horri-
fying as it is, is neither uncommon nor the worst that took place.

I prefer this story to others as its bitterness is mixed with joy and
relief, for three days after Wissam had been handcuffed and left
to die under the ground, acquaintances of his led some American
soldiers to a place in the road where they were convinced he had
been buried, and the soldiers dug away the cement and eventually
released Wissam, setting him free. He was convinced that the
soldiers were going to kill him, not understanding what was going
on and believing that he was being brought up from his tomb to
be shot. As he trembled and lowered his head in absolute fear, the

soldiers released his handcuffs, and with a translator at his side he was able to recount what had happened to him.

Wissam and his family now live in a mould-ridden apartment in Jordan. Until we were able to provide basic appliances and mattresses, they all slept in a row on the stone-cold floor, each with a cushion for their heads. They had no blankets, no belongings, no spare clothes – absolutely nothing. All they had was one another and their lives, and still this is the case. Each month we visit them, and they are one of the key families we provide for with the help and support of Messengers of Peace, the charity run by our associate priest, Father Kahlil. They have no ornaments or pictures – there was nothing to bring with them to Jordan from Baghdad as everything they owned was destroyed – but they do have a small framed picture of Jesus on their wall. In their words, as in the words of so many of my people, 'Yeshua is all we have.' Their children attend our school, and when we ask their parents about their situation they say that now, without jobs or business or any occupation, they love and appreciate each other more than they ever did. The bond of love that one can sense both within and emanating from these families is profound.

It is almost impossible to reflect on the story of Wissam's escape without pondering on the body of Jesus being in the tomb for three days and the mighty resurrection that followed. Similarly, one considers the great miracle of Lazarus, the close friend of Jesus who was called forth from the tomb. Within all of the tragedies that I could recount, the mercy, grace and redemptive love of the Almighty somehow blaze stronger than gunshots, explosions and earthly fire. As such, even if Wissam's story had never been told, his relationship with the God who rolled away the stone, his eternity with the risen Christ and his assurance of eventually being reunited with his loved ones would have remained unchanged. It is this higher perspective that enables my people to endure and to hold on to their faith in times of great suffering.

Even now, as part of a homeless, marginalized worshipping community in Jordan, so many of my people have learned how to break free from the dark clouds of oppression, sorrow and hardship that have weighed upon them. How do they do this? They simply allow the reality of Jesus and their love of Jesus to expand into a more concrete reality than the one they are experiencing.

In truth, they follow the example of Paul and Silas, who 'escaped from the tomb' and broke free of their chains due to the power of their praise and worship of the Almighty.[1] My people love to sing, shout and dance. Many described our 6,000-strong congregation in St George's Baghdad as the most joyful community they had ever visited. This joy was an eternal supernatural joy that came simply from being in the presence of the Almighty, and it continues to be their strength in the darkest times. As with Paul and Silas, their praise and worship create a door of escape from the prison cells of isolation and suffering. The effect of worship is not a simple, quick solution that instantly overrides the deep trauma and the suffering caused by persecution and the sense of loss and grief at every level, but it is indeed a very real weapon against depression and despair and a very real reason to say, recalling the popular song, that with Jesus we can face tomorrow.

In chapter 20 of 2 Chronicles, we learn of one of Judah's great kings, King Jehoshaphat, who knew exactly what to do in a time when the enemy forces were overwhelming. He gathered the nation's families and he exhorted them to fix their eyes on the one true God and to raise up anthems to praise, thank and adore him. As a result of this act, their story changed. Whether in this life, or in preparation for the next, faith and worship will always change our story. The tomb is empty; there is hope and redemption for all. Therefore let us keep proclaiming the great anthem of the psalmists and of Jehoshaphat's people: 'Give thanks to the LORD, for his love endures for ever' (2 Chronicles 20.21).

Prayer

We thank you, God, that you are the chain-breaker and the great deliverer. We thank you for the great gift of salvation and for being our all-sufficient one. We love you and we worship you with all of our hearts. Amen.

---

1   See Acts 16.25–31.

36

Raising champions 1

DESPINA

Beat your ploughshares into swords and your pruning hooks
into spears. Let the weakling say, 'I am strong!'
(Joel 3.10)

I would like to introduce you to several true heroes of our ministry, all people who started their lives with little opportunity, yet were
transformed by the reality of God's presence. In themselves they were
not significant, yet all had an effect both on me and on the societies in
which they were living. Many faced physical challenges, as well as the
challenges and obstacles of living in war zones, yet they all enabled us
to realize the supernatural empowerment of the Almighty, the ability
to rise above our situations and limitations and to trust to God to
help us make the transition into the reality of light and hope.

I want to tell you about various individuals. To me the stories of
these people are particularly moving, as I was intimately involved
in many aspects of their lives.

Joseph the carpenter worked in central Bethlehem, and took care
of his little daughter Despina (his firstborn child), who is now in
her thirties. In 1994, when I met the family, she was seven years
old. Soon after birth, Despina began to manifest the symptoms of
Marfan syndrome, a congenital disorder affecting connective tissue.
Typically, people with this condition are taller than usual, and suffer
from scoliosis of the spine, optic conditions and spleen dysfunction.

It was obvious from a young age that the scoliosis was so severe
it was putting pressure on Despina's heart and lungs. The kind
of treatment she required was not available in Bethlehem, as the

Palestinian territories do not have the advanced level of healthcare to provide the intensive treatment necessary. Only a few hospitals could treat her, such as the Royal National Orthopaedic Hospital in Stanmore, in the UK, or the Providence Heart Institute in Oregon, or the Hadassah Medical Center in Jerusalem. Ironically, as a Palestinian, she did not qualify for free treatment, despite the fact that one of the three top specialist hospitals in the world was effectively on her doorstep.

I decided to find the funding to pay for Despina's treatment. We needed $100,000 and were supported by the Barnabas Fund, of which I was the chairman at the time.[1] The Hadassah hospital carried out extensive tests and came up with a serious treatment plan, concluding that the only way to save her life was radical surgery involving the insertion of Harrington rods in order to straighten her vertebrae. Each vertebra had to be operated on, in order to align them with one another.

I had to guarantee that the money could be found quickly, as Despina's chance of survival was very limited. We had a huge amount of prayer support from Christians around the world, interceding for her healing and survival. The story was shared through our own network and that of the Barnabas Fund. Incredible financial assistance came through and the surgery went ahead. One of the very key people who helped us was Petra Ieldt, who has been a German Lutheran pastor in Jerusalem for over 30 years. She has been an important figure in the development of relationships between the Jewish and Christian worlds, including ancient Christian communities, especially the Syrian Orthodox community in which Despina's father (Joseph the carpenter) was a church leader. Together we aimed to do everything to support Despina and her family.

Petra herself was no stranger to suffering. She had been present at the scene of a terrible explosion in Jerusalem in the Mahane Yehuda market (the Jewish *souk*). She required extensive surgery and spent many weeks in intensive care at the Hadassah hospital, developing key relationships with many of the medical staff there.

---

1   The Barnabas Fund works to provide hope and aid for the persecuted Church.

During this time, Petra had much high-profile attention from the media and was involved in various TV programmes. She was held in exceptional regard and able to play a major role in assuring that Despina received the correct medical expertise. Petra's presence really accelerated the process.

The surgery was a great success. Despina spent several weeks in intensive care but recovered fully. She is now a graduate of the medical university with a degree in nursing and has recently achieved a master's in neonatal intensive care. She had further corrective surgery on her eyes and has been a great help to others in Israel-Palestine who have had serious congenital disorders.

Joseph, her father, became very involved in the Red Crescent organization, the Arab equivalent of the Red Cross, and regularly provided acute medical care to Palestinian victims of terror through the Palestinian Red Crescent.

After Despina's treatment was completed, I asked Joseph how else we could help him, and he immediately asked for a school. There was no school for the Syrian Orthodox churches in Bethlehem, despite the size of the community. Once again, working with the generous people who had supported Despina, we were able to raise funds to start a school. Hanna, Joseph and I spent many hours visiting all the possible properties that we could buy for this purpose. Eventually we identified a good single-storey building which would provide opportunity for development. The work commenced and within a few months we were ready to establish a kindergarten. The new Syrian Orthodox school would be known as Mar Ephrem School, in Beit Jala, the neighbouring town to Bethlehem.

One of the first children to enrol in the kindergarten was Despina's younger sister, Lara, known as Lulu.

Prayer

We thank you, God, that you are the great builder; that when things fall apart you are the God who rebuilds and restores. We thank you that from the dry barren places and the war zones of yesterday you have raised up new saplings, whose lives are a testimony to your great presence in our midst. Amen.

37
Raising champions 2

CHILDREN OF THE SIEGE

For He established a testimony in Jacob and appointed a law in Israel, which He commanded our fathers to teach to their children, that the coming generation would know them – even children yet to be born – to arise and tell their own children, that they should put their confidence in God, not forgetting His works, but keeping His commandments. (Psalm 78.5-7 BSB)

As I mentioned earlier in this book, a very key period for me, which actually gave birth to my international reconciliation ministry, was the siege of the Church of Nativity in Bethlehem in the spring of 2002, during which large areas of Bethlehem were under a curfew for 40 days.

It was particularly tough for newborn babies during this time. Their parents did not have sufficient food for the children. Some were being breastfed by malnourished mothers, while others were being prematurely weaned. One of our major responsibilities was providing food for these young families. I grew very close to the children and they would eventually become the first pupils of our Bethlehem school. To this day the relationship with all the families remains special, and in 2018 we had the first graduation from the school: in other words, we had seen a whole generation through from babies to graduates. The feedback given by the pupils in their graduation speeches, and their gratitude to us and to their parents, was extremely moving.

All of these children have gained university places, and the West Bank Educational Board stated that children graduating from this school had achieved far higher exam results than those leaving another school in the West Bank. This is an incredible testimony to God's faithfulness towards praying and believing families who had lived through invasion, captivity and political hardship, yet had not deviated from their faith and their devotion to the Almighty.

Many of these children have stayed close to me and have all excelled in academic and musical achievements. Two who come to mind are Nathalie (known as Nunu) and Yacoub. Nathalie competed in various regional and national choral competitions, which led to her performing at the Conservatoire in Paris. Yacoub, the younger brother of Despina, also had a brilliant voice and became the 2017 winner of the popular TV show *Arab Idol*. This covered all the Arab countries, not just the Palestinian territories. Yacoub had been very active in the Syrian Orthodox Scout Movement, known for its excellence in performing with bagpipes, a tradition dating back to the Scottish Legion's presence in Palestine during the overthrow of the Ottoman Empire. Since his award Yacoub has become a significant international singer, performing in both the American and Arab music worlds. As a child, he had always been the young voice singing in Manger Square, Bethlehem, during the turning on of the lights on Christmas Eve. He was the chosen voice for all *three* Christmas eves, celebrated by the Western churches, the Orthodox churches and the Armenian churches.

I pray that these young people, whose voices have gone before them and who have been raised in Christian communities, will be among the worship leaders of the future. Our prayer is that they will be the worshippers and prophetic intercessors of future generations, as the central part of their story is the coming of the Messiah and the light shining in darkness. Our prayer is that all of our school graduates may continue in their walk with God and be a blazing light for the most famous offspring of Bethlehem, the King of Glory. For all of us, our children, whether they sing or not, are the voices of the future, and we must pray that they will be influencers of society and ambassadors of hope wherever their path leads.

One of the other young Bethlehem champions was Jusiana (known as Juju), who was so academically outstanding at school that she was selected to participate in an annual year-long exchange with a high school in West Virginia. Her excellent command of the English language and her exceptional skills in mathematics, music and theatre enabled her to succeed in this very rigorous selection process.

It was wonderful to have had the unique opportunity to be Juju's only international guest connected with Bethlehem during her exchange year. It so happened that I was in the USA and was able to fly across to take her out for dinner with her host family.

Lulu, the girl I mentioned in the last chapter as being the very first child to enrol in our kindergarten, was one of the first babies of the siege whom I had the honour of holding during her baptism. Lulu has also performed with distinction in her academic subjects, especially English, and her dream is to be a professional translator.

These young people from Bethlehem and Jordan, whom I continue to meet with every month, call themselves 'the Clan'. This stands for 'Chosen-Loved-and-Named'. I always remind them of how God sees them and of how he calls them his children and friends. They all wear a special coloured bracelet made by crafts-people in one of our refugee communities. Their faith is very sincere and strong, and they know the power of love.

My desire is that all of these precious lives we have rescued, nurtured and educated will become a powerful community of faith-filled believers who understand their identity in Jesus and are able to bring transformation to regions and nations. In this area of great conflict, we realize that the only hope is the person whose life began in Bethlehem and ended in resurrection from a Jerusalem tomb. The hope of divine favour, restoration and blessing lies in this reality.

Prayer

Lord God, our maker and redeemer, we give you thanks and praise for raising up champions within a place of devastation. We thank you for the glorious power of the cross that brings transformation, hope and vision to so many and enables them to make a difference. We pray that this will be a daily reality for all of us and for our young ones at home and across the world. Amen.

38
Raising champions 3

AUSTRALIA'S GOT TALENT

Through the praise of children and infants you have established a stronghold against your enemies, to silence the foe and the avenger.
(Psalm 8.2)

Of all our work in Iraq, one of the features that most stands out in my mind was our regular Monday morning visits to the Mother Teresa home for unwanted children. This was a home in Baghdad run by the Sisters of Charity, the order founded by Mother Teresa of Calcutta. The sisters all wore their white sari with blue stripes and we loved them all and knew them well. They had been in Baghdad since the early 1990s when Mother Teresa visited the city in person.

The main house was based in Karada, and the sisters and children lived in various properties while we were there, but whatever the location, the main objective of the home was to provide a safe living space for children who had been totally rejected. Many of these boys and girls were literally found on the streets, and a number had serious congenital abnormalities such as missing arms and legs. It is likely that some of these conditions were caused by the large amount of depleted uranium covering many of the bombs and mortars that had been dropped on Baghdad.[1]

---

1   This occurred not during the 2003 war, but in the course of the previous conflict known as Operation Desert Storm, provoked when Saddam Hussein invaded Kuwait in the early 1990s.

Most of the children probably came from a Muslim background, but they were cherished in the Christian community provided by the sisters, and were raised as Christians. Among the many children we engaged with over the years there were certain individuals who really stood out. From the first time I started visiting the home, two of the children were particularly dear to me and had a great effect on me: Ahmed and Emmanuel.

The two boys were considered brothers, although the paperwork was missing so we could not be certain. They were very close to each other, looked very similar and could well have been twins. Both had serious congenital deformities with no real arms or legs, but they managed to shuffle around and were always exceptionally happy. They had a strong faith, and brought great joy to us. They always gave more to my life than I gave to them, as joy is priceless! The boys were discovered as babies, left in a shoebox, and the information on their background was very limited. Both spoke exceptional English with an Indian accent which they had learned from the nuns who cared for them. Every time we visited, they would sing to us in English: 'Thank you very much, very very very much, thank you very very very very much.'

One day, when Emmanuel and Ahmed were about six or seven, we had the news that a wonderful lady from Australia had visited them. Her name was Moira Kelly and we knew little about her other than that she had a history of adopting children from very difficult backgrounds. She visited our children and returned again with the specific aim of taking Ahmed and Emmanuel to Australia. She wanted to adopt them and she was soon granted permission to take them with her back to Australia. This, I knew, was totally wonderful for the children, but part of me was deeply sad: these two little boys who were our great sign of hope were being taken away.

Australia, incidentally, is the one nation which has offered true hospitality to the Iraqi refugees. Even as I write, several refugee families from my congregation in Baghdad, currently living in Jordan, are gradually being granted entry into this great country.

We continued to pray for the boys, to thank God for them, but we did not hear any news of them until the airing of the TV show

Australia's Got Talent in 2010. Emmanuel was one of the competitors and he told his story, which was broadcast to the whole of Australia and became known around the world. He sang John Lennon's 'Imagine', and his beautiful voice, nurtured during his childhood with the nuns as he and his brother learned to sing in English to Jesus, was now being used to touch the nation.

While Emmanuel specialized in singing, Ahmed became a gifted swimmer, despite his physical limitations. He developed in this area to such an extent that he swam in the 2012 London Paralympics, representing Australia. He did extremely well and we are all very proud of him. These boys are two of the greatest youth champions from the chaos of Baghdad. We thank God that they provide a wonderful example of what can be achieved with God's help and of the deep power of adoption, both physically and spiritually. Moira Kelly is herself a champion for adopting those who had been rejected.

This is the very essence of God's activity. He chose us and placed on us the spirit of adoption. In all our weakness he is strong. In our times of failure God empowers us to rise above every limitation, just as these boys have done.

Prayer

Lord God, we thank you that you have called us to be your champions, and have taken us out of darkness into your glorious light. We thank you that you are the Father of a family and that your heart is always to place those without families into a family. We thank you that in our weaknesses you are strength. Amen.

39
Raising champions 4

JUMANA

He took her by the hand and said, 'My child, get up!' Her spirit returned, and at once she stood up.
(Luke 8.54–55)

Jumana Copty Mansoor is another exceptional young friend.

From Jerusalem, she was a member of the Coptic (Egyptian) Christian community. I was first introduced to her by Archbishop Anba Abraham, the Coptic Archbishop of Jerusalem. He was one of my many close friends among the Jerusalem religious leaders, and had a significant leadership role among the city's archbishops. I would often go and sit with him in his apartment. Caroline and my sons also regularly visited him and on one occasion had a portrait painted with him which remained the main picture in his salon until he died in 2016.

On one of my many visits he pleaded with me to provide an internship for one of the young people in his community, so that she could come to England and spend a few months working with us. His young protégée, Jumana, was potentially a very good student and could be useful to us in our community. Her English was fluent, she had several pertinent skills, and had a place at the Hebrew University to train as a teacher after her gap year working with us. We accepted her as an intern, paid for her to come over and arranged for her to live with my family in Coventry. She had some relatives in the UK and related well to the Coptic community in Birmingham.

After her internship she returned to Jerusalem, where we maintained a close connection with her. She commenced at the

Hebrew University, reading English and Education, and did very well. However, just a few months into her first year of study she began to develop quite serious upper respiratory tract problems. I was in Israel at that point and decided she needed proper clinical treatment. She was thus admitted to the emergency medical unit at the Hadassah hospital. Within hours her situation further deteriorated, and she began to develop pneumonia. It quickly became obvious that her situation was so serious that she needed ventilating. She was thus intubated and put on a respirator.

At first the nature of the pneumonia was unclear. Various cultures were taken and the medical team eventually realized that she had a strange form of anaerobic bacterial infection. All sorts of intravenous antibacterial therapy were used to treat the infection, but there was very little response. Eventually it was clear that there was no quick solution, and a tracheotomy was performed.[1] Throughout all of this time I was praying for Jumana, continually at her bedside.

Her situation, however, continued to deteriorate and she required serious surgery for the removal of part of one of her lungs, as well as her spleen and part of a kidney. Jumana was by now suffering from very serious septicaemia. Many friends joined us in prayer, including leaders of different faiths, the Chief Rabbi, the Grand Imam and several of the patriarchal archbishops: all came and prayed for Jumana at the hospital.

For 40 days Jumana was in a critical condition. Then on day 41 the infection appeared to be coming under control. The septicaemia was diminishing, and to my total surprise she was taken off the ventilator and started to regain consciousness, all in the course of that single day.

Over the following days she made gradual progress. I stayed praying with her every day, and within a few more days she was finally able to communicate with us. As Jumana went through a long process of rehabilitation, she constantly gave thanks to God

---

1 A tracheotomy is an operation where an opening is created at the front of the neck so that a tube can be inserted into the trachea, to help the person breathe.

for his mercy and restoration. A few months later she was back at university, where the teaching staff allowed her to recommence the year.

After many years I am still in close contact with Jumana and she remains a friend of our team. Today she is a successful teacher in a very good Israeli school just outside Jerusalem.

This was indeed another story of great divine mercy and rescue, and a further example of how God intervenes in desperate situations in order to bring hope and allow people to fulfil both their dreams and his call upon their lives. This story has been one of the very powerful demonstrations to us of the wonder and might of the God we serve.

One of the memorable aspects of Jumana's situation was that as an intern she had regularly visited Yasser Arafat with me, and he continued to show very real concern about her development. He regularly phoned for an update on her while she was ill, and as soon as she had recovered and left hospital, one of the first things we did was to take her to see him. When he saw the incredible way she had been restored, he said, 'This is the work of my Jesus from Bethlehem.' He often said this when I shared with him the great acts of God's mercy within our work and community.

Prayer

We thank you, God, for your healing power and your mercy. We thank you that you are the great restorer. We pray that Jumana's testimony of being taken from tragedy to victory will be a story that brings hope to many and repeats itself in the lives of others whose health is diminishing and who need your very present help in time of need. Amen.

40

Raising champions 5

YOUSSEF AND THE JORDAN SCHOOL

He heals the broken-hearted and binds up their wounds.
(Psalm 147.3)

Soon after I left Baghdad during the ISIS uprising, we had news of tragic attacks on the family of one of the boys from our youth group – Youssef. His father had been killed for refusing to renounce his Christian faith, and Youssef had had oil thrown over him and then been set on fire.

This young boy went through various emergency procedures in Iraq as the doctors tried to deal with some of the main injuries to his head, neck, shoulders, arm and abdomen, including the removal of part of his ear. He underwent extensive reconstructive surgery and skin grafts. This meant he was out of school for at least four years, during which he knew intense physical and emotional pain. As soon as he was stabilized, his mother was determined to move the family away from Iraq and they came to Jordan, taking refuge among the Christian Iraqi community there. Soon after arriving in Jordan I reunited with him at our clinic in Amman, where we were able to give him further necessary treatment. Unfortunately, we did not have enough money to cover the additional reconstructive surgery Youssef required. Various possible sources of funding proved fruitless.

As Youssef's health continued to improve, we made a place available for him at our school so that he could integrate himself within the young Iraqi Christian community, receive education and develop plans for his long-term future. His return to school was a deeply moving event, timed to correspond with the arrival of me and my team in Jordan. The entire school assembled in the courtyard to pay tribute to the young hero, and many young faces looked reflective as they knew only too well that members of their own families had been the victims of similar violence, walked through similar storms, and known similar sorrow and grief. Nevertheless, as the welcome speech was given and Youssef was blessed, the atmosphere turned to one of celebration and hope, and thanks were given for the fact that his life had been spared. I was able to have some private time with him to pray with him, anoint him and give him some gifts. As he put on his new uniform and collected his pack of stationery and books, we saw a glimmer of hope and relief on his face. The memories were still harrowing, but the page of Youssef's life was turning and a new chapter about to be written.

It is not the end of the story yet. There is a lot that still needs to be achieved and further ongoing surgery will be necessary. Youssef is now having special classes in English and information technology among our older children, as we want them to have the required computer skills for work in the modern world.

One of the key subjects in Jordanian schools is the learning of Scripture, not least because memorizing the Qur'an word by word is a basic aspect of Islamic education. The Christian community in Jordan therefore goes through a similar system of learning the New Testament word for word in Arabic. In the light of this custom, all of our own schoolchildren regularly learn and have competitions for memorizing the New Testament. Our school has taken great pride recently in gaining the highest marks in the national inter-school competition.

Central to this initiative was learning the Bible from our small solar-powered audio MegaVoice Bibles. These were first given to us by Northern Irish friends whom we met in Jerusalem. The Bibles are supplied by the international charity MegaVoice, and have proved invaluable when so many of the Bibles belonging to the Christians in Iraq were destroyed by ISIS. Given the power of the Middle Eastern sun, and the fact that Jordanian methods of school testing are verbal as well as written, we had the perfect methodology in our hands to allow children to easily absorb the Scriptures without imposing on them endless hours of heavy reading. The very thing that ISIS had thus sought to destroy (the word of God, our greatest hope and weapon) had not only been redeemed to us by a distant charity, but was now the very reason our scholars were being viewed as national champions. For many of us, this was a great symbol of how God is able to reverse and restore. On a spiritual level, that which the enemy tried to steal was now being fired back at him through the mouths of mere infants. As we know, the word of God is powerful and imperishable.

One of the wonderful things about this whole process was that these solar audio Bibles had been presented to us in English *and* Arabic, so the children also used them as a means of improving their English, vital for those being granted asylum in English-speaking countries.

Once again, so much of what the enemy meant for harm was turning to good, and all things were starting to work together for the benefit of our people. Winning this national contest not only improved the corporate standard of English within our school; it also raised our students' confidence and self-esteem, and established their identity as winners, not losers. This change in self-perspective was evident among the staff as well as the pupils.

Prayer

We thank you, Father, that you are the healer and the provider. We ask that you will raise up Youssef and his friends to be a powerful voice for your glory within his generation.

We receive your saving grace and your divine favour, and we thank you for the power of your word which is eternal and sustaining – the greatest treasure of all. Amen.

41

Raising champions 6

THE SINGERMANS

He proclaimed the kingdom of God and taught about the Lord
Jesus Christ – with all boldness and without hindrance!
(Acts 28.31)

Young people have always been an inspiration to me.

I first met Sarah Singerman when she was a student at 'Gateway
and Beyond' in Cyprus – a small ministry training school. The
college had been founded by a Messianic Jew, and brings together
Jewish believers and others from around the world in order to train
and equip them to be leaders. Its focus is on Israel and the Jewish
people, and on building bridges between the Church and Israel.
It is also involved in worship, prayer and revival, as well as ministry to the poor, with focused outreach into Ethiopia and Ukraine.
Since I belonged to the Diocese of Cyprus and the Gulf at the time,
I always ensured that whenever I attended a diocesan synod on the
island, I visited the college. Each time I was there, various students
inspired me, and over the years I developed close relationships with
some of these young people, who would often come on short-term
placements with me.

One year I was impressed by a young American student called
Sarah Singerman. I knew little about her, but often prayed with her
and gradually learned of her family's own history. The family had
spent a considerable time living in Cyprus engaged in missionary
work, and it was from there that they decided to make *aliya* and
emigrate to Israel. Sarah graduated from the college and returned
to Israel, where she began her military service. Due to the excellent

standard of her English and her fine communication skills, she was given a significant position, responsible for communicating the vision and practices of the Israeli Defence Force to the outside world and media.

Following Sarah's return from her college in Cyprus, I had remained in contact and became very close to the whole family, regularly spending Erev Shabbat[1] with them in Abu Ghosh. This is one of the few small Arab towns in Israel where all the Arab residents are committed to the state of Israel. Many have served in the IDF because they are very peace-promoting people and have historically always been highly supportive of Israel. They see themselves as more Israeli than Palestinian. Sarah's family were quite unique in being such a Jewish presence in an almost exclusively Arab community. Often I would stay in their guest house, which was a wonderful opportunity to meet many international guests who, like us, had a passion for both Jews and Arabs.

During Sarah's time in the Israeli army she always took every opportunity to talk to her fellow soldiers about her faith in Jesus the Messiah and how Jesus was their means of salvation. She was often asked deep and complex questions, and always gave thanks to God that she had the chance to share the truth of the gospel. This approach of sharing the truth within a military context truly makes Sarah a champion, for in essence she has become a missionary to the heart of the Israeli army. There were occasions when I visited her at her military base in Jerusalem. It was phenomenal to see the great respect shown to her by her colleagues and how close to them she had become – to such an extent that her military commanders granted permission for her friend, 'a Christian priest', to enter the base and visit her. This was almost unheard of, as was the level of boldness and courage that Sarah had shown in her desire to stand as a voice for her Messiah.

Of the seven Singerman children, the one I grew particularly fond of was Yoshi. Yoshi, as a young boy, played a significant role in my life and ministry.

---

1   Hebrew for 'Sabbath Eve'.

It started when his dear mother had her latest child, a little girl called Sherea. Yoshi was very sad that there were now four female children and only three boys in the family: he felt outnumbered! I therefore assured him that I had some adopted boys and that one of them, called Amar, could become his brother. So Amar from Iraq became his close friend, and they talked and prayed together regularly on the phone.

I would often buy the family Jewish gifts, and when Yoshi reached the age for his bar mitzvah I was involved in the event and the ceremony, which took place at the Western Wall, and was able to buy his tefillin (phylacteries) from Mea Shearim, a venerable corner of Jerusalem. It was wonderful to hear him speaking of his real encounter with the Messiah. Yoshi grew up praising and praying every day, and stood out in the Jewish community for his boldness as a follower of Yeshua.

I watched him grow up. He even came to give a speech at the school of reconciliation that we hold each year at Jerusalem, where he spoke of his Iraqi brother and of his love for the Arab people. Many of my international guests met him and were inspired by him. By the age of ten he was advising me to organize a forum to officially bring together the Israelis and Iraqis. We could not do it in Israel or Iraq, so he had the idea of holding the meeting in Cyprus, the only other land that he knew well.

This turned out to be not just a sweet idea from the mouth of a child eager to help, but a case of key direction from heaven. The prayers and intercessions of Yoshi and his family played a pivotal role in the event. A venue was found and a huge process of planning took place. Yoshi, by then 11 years of age, was part of the official delegation, along with major figures from the Jewish, Muslim and Christian communities: rabbinic leaders; Shia and Sunni leaders, including ayatollahs; and bishops, patriarchs and other senior leaders of various denominations, including the Assyrian Church of the East. There were also high-ranking political representatives from both sides. Here was this young boy being the champion behind the conception and execution of the first ever major religious meeting between Israel and Iraq.

Yoshi's father also accompanied him, and this itself was significant as it was highly unusual for an important Messianic Jewish leader to be seen among serious orthodox rabbinic authorities and ayatollahs. Though not actually present in the meetings themselves, Yoshi played a unique reconciliatory role between members of the different groups, using breaks and mealtimes to interact with them. He had no experience, knowledge, education or adult maturity, but he was an expert at getting alongside individuals and becoming their friends. He did this to such an extent that many of the Iraqi leaders vied to sit next to him at dinner. He worked with Arabic and Hebrew translators, and his ideas and insights were well developed for a boy of that age. Yoshi was also instrumental in overseeing the 24-7 Prayer Room in Paphos, the town where we met. This room was directly above where we were gathered, and prayers took place there while the meetings were happening.

At the end of the forum, one of the chief rabbis stated that 'fear is cancelled', and he thanked Yoshi for being a key part of the event.

I hope and pray that this young champion will be endowed with great wisdom, and will continue to be a true reconciler for the sake of the kingdom.

Prayer

We thank you, God, that you are the ultimate peacemaker. You are perfect love, and perfect love casts out all fear. We thank you that when things seem impossible you provide the strategies and solutions that open doors of opportunity. We thank you for orchestrating events and bringing people together so that friendships can be established. Amen.

42

Walls

When the trumpets sounded, the army shouted, and at the sound of the trumpet, when the men gave a loud shout, the wall collapsed; so everyone charged straight in, and they took the city.
(Joshua 6.20)

Walls have been very significant in my life and ministry, all of them in different contexts and situations. The first walls that came to my attention were none other than the walls of Jericho. Like many of us who grew up attending Sunday school, I always enjoyed the great dramatic narratives of the Bible, and one of my favourites was the exciting story of Joshua and the walls of Jericho. The whole notion of city walls was always of great interest to me, as in England we had various cities with ancient Roman and medieval remains. Of course, I did not realize during my early years that Jericho would one day be a very meaningful part of my life.

In my early days of travelling to Israel-Palestine I would often go to Jericho and visit the monastery on the Mount of Temptation. My memories of these visits are very vivid, especially the joy of walking in the Palestinian desert. As my work in the Middle East developed, Jericho became a very significant place within my reconciliation work. The most important thing for me was that it was the home town of Saeb Erekat. He was Yasser Arafat's chief peace negotiator and as such I had to go there regularly to see him.

Today I still visit Jericho frequently, not simply for the nurturing of relationships but also for the purchase of local dates. The dates grown in Jericho are truly quite spectacular and unlike those produced anywhere else in the world.

When I have time alone in Jericho to contemplate and meditate, my thoughts often centre on two biblical aspects: the faithfulness and power of God in enabling the united sound of jubilee to cause ancient walls to collapse; and the healing and restorative ministry of Jesus on the road to Jericho. Wherever my thoughts go as I ponder the Scriptures, the power of God for incredible breakthrough and the ability of God to solve insurmountable problems is always a reality that ministers to my heart.

The next wall that I became very acquainted with was the Berlin Wall. While I was a student at Cambridge University, I became the chairman of the Young Leadership section of the International Council of Christians and Jews. That council was based in Germany, so I spent a lot of time working there before the fall of the Wall in 1989. Much of our interfaith work was in Berlin, on both sides of the wall, so that forbidding structure became a familiar part of my life.

The great historical date that one will never forget is 8 November 1989, the date of the fall of the Berlin Wall, when the barrier between East and West Germany was broken down and Germany was united. I remember that day so well. I was in my room in Cambridge studying the theologian Friedrich Schleiermacher, whose work I found somewhat tedious and uninspiring. The extremely dramatic and eventful unfolding of this truly pivotal moment was a matter of great joy, and it made a fairly average and mundane day come alive with excitement and celebration.

The other significant walls in my journey have been the Western Wall at the temple remains in Jerusalem; the security wall/fence between Israel and the West Bank; and finally the walls in Baghdad separating the Red Zone (normal Baghdad) from the Green Zone (fortified secure Baghdad). The Western Wall, the remains of the Second Temple in Jerusalem, is for me a deep source of inspiration. The wall is popularly known in Hebrew as the Kotel. Prior to the Six Day War in 1967, it was often referred to as the 'Wailing Wall', as it was here that people would come and lament over the division of Jerusalem and over the fact that the ruins of the Holy Temple were not truly accessible. To be there nowadays on Friday night is a deeply inspiring and thought-provoking experience as people dance to the 'songs of Zion'.

The next wall in my life can be seen from the Western Wall. It is not a source of joy but a source of great pain. It is the separating wall or fence between Israel and the West Bank. The purpose of this barrier was to prevent terrorists getting into Israel, and though its purpose has largely been achieved, the harsh reality is that it has divided families, torn apart entire communities and cut through many Palestinian people's farms. The pain this wall has generated has been awful, and demonstrates so much of the agony caused by conflict and terror.

So often in society, walls of separation are set in place and their existence causes divisions to multiply. Sadly, there is no easy solution. Communities, cities, regions and whole nations that should be one and at peace with each other are divided and become enemies. Walls that create separation often lead to hatred, rivalry and violence. In part of Baghdad the wall of separation is in fact the River Tigris. On one side of the river is the Shia area of Kadhimiya, the location of the great Shia shrine of the al-Kadhimiya Mosque, containing the shrine of Imam al-Kazim; while across the river lies the Sunni area of Adhamiya, which is in reality a Sunni intellectual hotspot for rich and famous professionals. The two communities are geographically close, but the divide is not a mere river: it is religious identity. Shia and Sunni communities are so near to each other but so far apart ethnically, culturally and religiously.

The other divides of Baghdad are the separation barriers. These consist of huge concrete blocks, placed as protection around secure areas. Baghdad is divided into two zones. The Green Zone is the secure area where the embassies are found, as well as the Parliamentary Assembly and government buildings. For many years I lived just outside the Green Zone, in the Red Zone, which is the normal unsecure area where the masses live. Even within the Red Zone there would be specific areas marked by additional walled sections, which provided further security. Among the shrines and 'holy' sites, there were thus walls and barriers that signalled the existence of a tension that was anything but holy.

I realize that I am talking about visits to sites in Iraq where very few people will have ever been, apart from some high-profile journalists. I feel privileged to have been able to see and discover so much about the history of the land.

Both Jerusalem and Baghdad are places of great biblical and historical significance, places where God moved so evidently among his people; yet today they are places of disunity and conflict. As the Friday jubilation at the Western Wall in Jerusalem rings out, just across the Wall is Haram al-Sharif (the Temple Mount), which visibly represents the depth of the rift between the communities of this famous city.

My prayer is that as labourers and peacemakers are sent forth, we will see walls and obstacles start to dissolve, and that those who once lived in conflict and hatred will come to know cooperation, reconciliation and peace in their time.

Prayer

Lord, we pray that you will enable all of us to bring down walls in our families, neighbourhoods, communities, societies and regions. We pray that where there is division, there may be unity and reconciliation. Help us to play our part to unite people in love and friendship. Amen.

43
Faith and hope

We have this hope as an anchor for the soul, firm and secure. It enters the inner sanctuary behind the curtain, where our forerunner, Jesus, has entered on our behalf. He has become a high priest for ever, in the order of Melchizedek.
(Hebrews 6.19-20)

The very heart of the book of Hebrews teaches on faith and hope. Hope is what always keeps us going. It stops us giving up. Hope is the anchor that keeps us steady in the storm.

This hope is linked to the Temple by the sacrificial and mystical high-priest figure of Jesus, the one who was and is and is to come. This falls in line with the name of God that I will never say or write, but a name that is past, present and future. It is the Holy Name, too holy ever to be said or written in full.

So the very heart of Judaism is reverence for the Holy Name, and this passage about faith has at its very heart the whole concept of hope. Where there is faith, there is always hope. Hope in the eternal one who has no beginning or end - the great messianic figure who was and is and is to come; the anointed one, who is also our Jesus.

This is our hope. What are we truly hoping for? All of us hope to be free from the things that cause us pain and suffering. The things that cause this are countless. It could be physical pain and illness, which we or those we love are enduring. So often in my life, it is emotional pain: being keenly aware of the suffering of others whom we deeply love or care about. This pain is often to do with loss. Not just loss of health, but loss of freedom, control, independence. The hope of which Hebrews speaks is that very soon things will be different. The hope is in our Lord Jesus, who will one day come and stand beside us, bless us and anoint us, and cause us to be more like him in his resurrected form.

To be there with Jesus in his resurrected glory not only means to be in the presence of our God, but also means to be away from all fears and from the presence of the evil one. That is the hellish life we need to escape from. Our certain hope is that with God we will. That does not mean we will all be supernaturally healed and equipped, though we know God can certainly do that. What it does mean is that the Lord will always be beside us. I know he always will be with me and he will always sustain me. The fact that our Lord is always beside us is what enables us to know we are not on our own. None of us likes to be alone. We all need times of quietness when we can pray and reflect, but we also need times with others.

I have to confess I am a radical extrovert. I need others and am empowered by them. I am the kind of person who can be surrounded by people all the time and love it. Often people have said to me that it must be so difficult, being incessantly surrounded by others. For me it is not difficult: it is wonderful! As much as I am an extrovert, my dear wife is an introvert; she finds it hard when I am at home and there are endless streams of people coming to see me. I am trying to be more sensitive about this issue.

We do indeed have a hope that is secured with that great anchor who is Christ our Lord. The great anchor keeps us secure in our commitment to the service of our Lord. In the course of my life and ministry, dealing with people who are often more concerned with war than peace, it is my Lord Jesus who has always been my anchor and has kept me secure in my journey of faith.

As a boy I was a member of the Boys' Brigade, a youth body similar to the Scout Movement, but very much rooted in the Christian faith. Its symbol was an anchor, and our theme hymn was 'Will Your Anchor Hold':

Will your anchor hold in the storms of life,
When the clouds unfold their wings of strife?

When the strong tides lift, and the cables strain,
Will your anchor drift or firm remain?

We have an anchor that keeps the soul
Steadfast and sure while the billows roll,
Fastened to the Rock which cannot move,
Grounded firm and deep in the Saviour's love.
(Priscilla Jane Owens, 1829–1907)

I grew up knowing how significant our Lord was as the anchor. In the turbulent life I endure, I delight that my Lord is indeed the anchor that keeps me 'steadfast and sure while the billows roll'.

Prayer

Lord God, we thank you that you are our unending hope. We thank you that you are our anchor that will always keep us secure. Keep us firm in our unending love and service of you.

O Lord, we love you so much. Amen.

44

The Lord is here

The Lord is the Spirit, and where the Spirit of the Lord is, there
is freedom.
(2 Corinthians 3.17)

Central to much of what I do and say are these words, which
feature regularly in the Anglican liturgy, notably in the Eucharist:
'The Lord is here and his Spirit is with us.' Often I find myself saying
these words, usually when things seem so good that I know the events
are inspirational and supernatural. In the good times, the wonderful
times, God is present. As I write I am in Chicago. I have been speaking at an inspirational conference where the Lord was certainly there
and his Spirit was clearly with us. Yesterday morning, I was keenly
aware that the Lord was saying that today was going to be a great and
supernatural day. I said, 'Thank you, Lord.'

I did not know what would happen. Lots of Iraqis have taken
refuge in Chicago. One such person, called Joann, had contacted
me and said that she and her family wanted to see me. She said she
had not seen me for seven years. I badly wanted to meet her, but I
could not remember who she was.

We met at the hotel with her brother Martin and her parents.
When I saw her, I realized she was one of my dear young people
whom I called Juju. She showed me a picture of herself in one of my
books. It was the picture of her with me when we saw Jesus and the
angels. It was the day we saw the mega glory of God and the most
incredible image of Jesus that I have ever seen.

We sat and talked about the day we saw Jesus, a day we will both
never forget. It still has a major impact on both our lives. We did see
Jesus, and once you have seen him you will never forget it. That was

the first time I saw a vision of Jesus. The Lord was there and his Spirit was truly with us.

The other times when those words have been especially significant to me have often been when everything was awful. When those I loved had been killed, or there had been terrorist attacks. At such times all I could do was say, 'The Lord is here and his Spirit is with us.' Everything may have been terrible, frightening and serious, but I knew the Lord was still with me.

We all have times in our spiritual life and journey when we are aware of the presence of our Lord. We may not have seen him visually, but we have known for sure that he is there with us, constantly inspiring and comforting us.

It is now two days after the Chicago conference, and I am back in the Middle East with my Iraqi community in Jordan. This is the nearest I get to being home among my people. By my side as usual is Hanna from Jerusalem. Having an Israeli passport, he is not allowed into Iraq with me, but he has always been with me and my Iraqi people who fled to Jordan. Once again I am acutely aware that 'the Lord is here and his Spirit is with us'. That presence of the Lord does not go away. His presence changes our life to be what God wants. Our God is not only present; he is also transcendent. This means that life is not just about earth but about heaven, and in so much of my life I experience heaven come to earth.

We know that God is everywhere, but he is also here with us now. Whatever our circumstances, we know that the Lord is here and his Spirit is with us. There are seven clear aspects of the presence of God:

1 It means God is really near, and where God is, there is freedom.
2 It means God is listening to our prayers.
3 It means God is speaking to us.
4 It means that God's glory is around us.
5 That glory means that all his power is made available to us.
6 In his power we are to be his hands and his feet.
7 We are nothing less than his supernatural glory-bearers; the channels of his majesty.

So the Lord is Spirit, and where the Spirit of the Lord is, there is freedom. That freedom is a major part of the presence of God. Freedom at its very heart means freedom from the presence of fear. There can be so many causes of fear; I have looked at many in this book. The result of this freedom is always liberty. Once again, when one looks at liberty, one has to look at a huge variety of aspects of being released to be what God wants you to be and wants you to experience. Liberty is indeed to do with living in the presence of God in all its fullness.

So we live in the presence of the glory and majesty of the Almighty, in a liberty and power that totally transcends what we could even imagine.

Prayer

We thank you, Lord, for your liberty. We thank you, Lord, for your freedom. We thank you, Lord, that in your presence there is glory. We thank you, Lord, that in your glory there is unending power. We thank you, Lord God. Amen.

45

Rising like the sun

So may all your enemies perish, O Lord!
But may all who love you be like the sun
when it rises in its strength.
(Judges 5.31)

In writing the chapters of this book of meditations, I have mainly chosen my favourite verses and meditated on them at length. I did, however, ask three people to whom I am very close if each would give me his or her favourite verses to reflect and write on, and today's reading is one of them. I must confess it was a total surprise when one of my friends and colleagues suggested to me this favourite verse of theirs, taken from the book of Judges. It is a part of Scripture that I have, of course, read, but never before really studied or preached on.

To me, this book of Judges is one of the most difficult in the Bible. It makes the book of Lamentations look like a Sunday school hymn. So before I talk about the verse in question, I want to look briefly at the background to the book of Judges.

It gives no indication as to who the author is. However, in the Jewish rabbinic world, it is widely presumed to be written by the prophet Samuel, last of the 'judges' of Ancient Israel. These judges did not oversee merely legal matters, as in our sense of the role; their tasks often included military and administrative authority as well. In those early days there was no king, so these individuals also held kingly authority and were looked to as rulers, and they were raised up by God to rescue his people. The author of Judges lived in the early days of the establishment of the monarchy; he states several times, 'In those days there was no king.' The book of Judges looks as if it was written before David was appointed king in Jerusalem in 1004 BC, yet after Saul was appointed king in 1051 BC. So it would seem that Judges begins after the death of Joshua (see Joshua 24.29) and continues until the crowning of Saul by Samuel.

Judges tells the story of many of the Hebrew tribes in several different areas. It was a time of huge trial, conflict and controversy as various groups tried to take control of territory that was not yet theirs. The result was a period of great intertribal violence, disbelief and even idolatry. This radical, dramatic cycle of conflict kept repeating itself. Despite this great tragedy, we also meet here many great heroes of the faith, such as Gideon, Samson, Ehud, Jephthah and, of course, dear Deborah.

The key message of this difficult book is that God does not allow sin to go unpunished. God is the ultimate judge and person of justice, and so we come to the words of Deborah in our verse:

So may all your enemies perish, O LORD!
But may all who love you be like the sun
when it rises in its strength.

Deborah was not just a great judge; she was also a prophet. She had been living amid turmoil and conflict but had one clear message, which was that the enemies of the Lord would be against God and that he would cause them to perish. So often, tragically, there are people who think they are fighting for God when in fact they are fighting against him.

Deborah was a great prophetic figure, and she declared that the greatest thing in life was to love, love and love the Lord. When surrounded by stress, conflict and turbulence, it is so easy to give up and think that nothing can be done. Deborah shows us that this can never be the answer, for those who love God will rise in the strength of the Son – in supernatural, spiritual strength. That strength and love will prevail, and overcome the powers of evil and darkness. Light and love really do go together, and together they will overcome.

Deborah is also a lesson for us all as to how God wants to use women as his powerful weapons and tools. Don't ever think that women are weak and can't deliver, for here God shows us that in great turmoil and opposition it is a woman whom he uses to bring justice, wisdom and wholeness. The song of Deborah is not just a song for women; it is a song for all those who faithfully love and serve God. The most wonderful thing about this song of Deborah is that she was with a partner, Barak, a man who was not actually her husband but nevertheless a man who shared with her the everlasting vision of the love and glory of the Almighty. God does not call us to serve alone, but promises always to provide the right person and people so that we can sing of his glory together.

Prayer

Lord, we shall sing of your love for ever. Our love shall be like your rising sun. Our strength will flow from you for ever.

Give us all our Deborah and Barak, so that we will always have partners as we sing your song. For Lord, we will indeed sing of your love for ever. Help us to always be your faithful servants. Amen.

46

The prayer of Jabez

Oh, that you would bless me and enlarge my territory! Let your
hand be with me, and keep me from harm so that I will be free
from pain.
(1 Chronicles 4.10)

We don't know much about Jabez. We know he wrote the above
prayer, and that he was from the tribe of Judah, but we don't
know anything more about his ancestry or lineage. We know that
his name means he was born in great pain. All we really have of
him is his prayer, where he calls on the God of Israel and says,
'Oh, that you would bless me and enlarge my territory! Let your
hand be with me, and keep me from harm so that I will be free
from pain.'

The first thing Jabez does is ask God to bless him. In other words,
he asks the Almighty to enable him to be all that God desires and
needs him to be. The prayer is a reminder to us all that we should
come to God sincerely, in our request for blessing, so that God can
anoint us and use us fully for the sake of his calling.

The second thing Jabez asks God for is to enlarge his territory, to
increase his responsibility and influence. This is indeed something
that we all should do continually: to ask for God's eternal presence
to increase our impact throughout our workplace, calling and
world. It has been very important to me in my own ministry where
I have continually asked the Lord to give me a greater span of influence and involvement. Central to my calling has been cooperation
with various heads of state, and international religious and political
leaders. My type of work has also included being led by God to the
key figures who are often involved in the cause of conflicts. This has

meant dealing not just with prime ministers and presidents but also with terrorists, as this book has shown.

Third, Jabez prays that God will be with him and stay close to him. And finally, he asks that God will keep him from harm and free from pain. Continually in my work and role as a priest, I have been faced with serious, often physical attacks which could have caused great pain and an ending to my ministry, but always I have experienced the intense supernatural presence of God, providing healing, safety and security.

This has also been the case in my ongoing journey with MS. As I write this chapter, it is Christmas Eve and I am in hospital, preparing to spend Christmas not with my family but miles away from them. Yet I know the presence of God is with me. Despite illness, suffering and pain, God enables us to continue our work and ministry. I have always said that one of the wonderful things about following God's desire for our lives is that he always gives us joy in doing what we are called to do. Despite the various tragedies and difficulties, there is sometimes freedom from pain, and the experience of joy, and that enables us to continue.

The amazing message in the prayer of Jabez is God's full provision: God providing for us in a miraculous way to enable us to do what he has called us to do. There is only one God and he should be the centre of our life and work, and he wishes to bless that work every day. But in order to live this ministry of supernatural power to the full, we need to invite the Almighty to increase his sphere of influence in our life, work and ministry on a daily basis.

This prayer of Jabez has been fundamental to my own life and ministry over the past decade, and I continually pray that God will enable these four points of expansion in my life. To move forward in this supernatural relationship with God, there must be a continuous close link with the Almighty, a daily intimate connection with our Lord and his Holy Spirit. Only then will we know him as the one who always provides for us and keeps us from pain and suffering.

Jabez demonstrates total dependence on God. His words remind us that we all struggle with desiring to rely totally on God, but we can be assured that he is always there with us, and will enable us to move forward and come into a deeper relationship with him.

The example of Jabez is of one who knows the Lord and yet wants to draw even closer in prayer. In order to do this, one requires an intimate and continual relationship with the Holy Spirit.

Jabez and his prayer should be a radical challenge to all of us to live a triumphant life, blessed with the gifts and power and provision of the Spirit of the living God. There are times when we all fail to live in the presence of God as he would want us to. This prayer of Jabez is one of our greatest reminders. Pray, ask, and live this prayer every day – and keep a record of the times when God answers your requests!

Prayer

O Lord, that you would bless me and enlarge my territory! Let your hand be with me and keep me from harm so that I will be free from pain. Amen.

47
Look for God

You will seek me and find me when you seek me with all your
heart.
(Jeremiah 29.13)

It was Christmas Day 2017. Somehow I had contracted
septicaemia, totally unrelated to the MS but making it a lot worse.
The difficulty was that the primary source of the infection was not
known. There appeared to be no infection in the lungs, bladder or
bowel, just a severe generalized infection of the blood. Our blood
affects our whole body, so all of me was feeling very unwell. I was
put on intravenous infusions of antibiotics, and after three days I
was well enough to start writing again. This chapter was the first
thing I wrote.

I felt so ill. I could not even pray properly, but I could still find
God because I had never lost him, so even though I was unable to
communicate much, I knew he was still with me. I do not need to
search for God because I have not lost him. As I say continually, the
Lord is here and his Spirit is with us.

On Christmas Day itself, I wanted to go to the hospital chapel
for Holy Communion. The problem was that I still wasn't feeling
well enough and didn't have anyone to take me in the wheelchair.
The nurses contacted the chaplaincy, and Chaplain Joanna came
to see me that morning. She said to me that she had certain words
of Scripture that were important to her at various times. I'm much
the same. On this particular day, the phrase in my mind was simply
'Look for God.'

It came as a challenge to me. Being in hospital, in a dry and boring room, it can sometimes seem as if God is nowhere to be found, and I decided that it should be the subject of this chapter:

- How do we look for God?
- What does it mean to find him?
- Where do we look?

Each of us must find our own path to encounter the reality of his presence.

First, most obviously, this can be in Scripture. We study the Bible and find the words of the prophets and the apostles, and those of Jesus himself.

We also find the presence of God in listening to those we respect and revere as great teachers of the word of God. This does not just mean great pastors and priests. It can be anyone we encounter with an exceptionally close relationship to the Almighty.

I think of many people from whom I've heard the word of God; some expected, some unexpected.

I think of Lord Donald Coggan, former Archbishop of Canterbury. He is a man I greatly revered, and to whose memory I have dedicated this book. He first taught me to take risks, and always showed me the presence of God.

I think of people around the world whom I have been greatly influenced by. I think of a young boy, only 11 years old, from Washington State, USA. I had just spoken in an assembly at his school when he came up to me and gave me one dollar, as a sign of what God wanted to do to meet our needs. I've seen that boy several times since. By giving me one dollar, he unknowingly showed me the presence of God.

Everywhere I went, I told the story of Sean giving me one dollar. So many people started giving me their one dollar, one dinar, one pound. In the end, that one dollar provided $4.7 million, before I stopped counting.

These are just two encounters with very different individuals who showed me the presence of God. Jeremiah 29, one of the most famous prophetic chapters, says: 'You will seek me and find me when you seek me with all your heart.' To seek God is to have a real desire to find the Almighty, to search for him in Scripture, through inspirational people, through contacts. Yet we cannot deny that in seeking there is always a supernatural element. God also speaks to us through the gifts of the Holy Spirit – through words of wisdom, knowledge, tongues and prophecy.

To receive such gifts is always awe-inspiring. When God speaks through us supernaturally, we sense God coming into our presence. This is the most direct way in which God talks and meets with us, and enables us to know his reality.

We think of the disciples' experience walking on the road to Emmaus after the death of Jesus. They were talking about how difficult life was going to be without his presence. It was at this low point of their lives, when they felt God was most distant from them and nowhere to be found, that God appeared to them.

They were joined by an unknown man, a traveller. He spoke to them and reassured them, gave them hope. The traveller tried to bid them farewell, but they were enjoying his presence and asked him to stay. The traveller accompanied them for the rest of their journey, but it was only when they broke bread with him at the end of the day that the disciples realized that this unknown man, who had so reassured them, was, in fact, Christ their Lord and Saviour. Their hearts and minds were filled with faith and hope.

Sometimes in life, we are comforted by unknown strangers. We find spiritual peace in places we never expected it. As with the disciples, this can happen when we feel most distant from God – in hospital, in the cemetery. But it is at times like these that God can appear to us, disguised in the wise and comforting words of strangers and friends. For all of us, there will be times when we experience the presence of God. We will not always understand how or why, but we will know that the Lord is there and his Spirit is with us.

Prayer

Lord, I am seeking you with all my heart. May I find you in the expected places and the unexpected places. Amen.

48
Jonah and Thomas

Who will not fear you, Lord, and bring glory to your name?
For you alone are holy. All nations will come and worship
before you, for your righteous acts have been revealed.
(Revelation 15.4)

Jonah, one of the great historical people of the Bible, is often
viewed negatively. Yet his very name means 'dove', which represents
peace and the Holy Spirit.

In Iraq, Jonah is considered one of the greatest saints. Mar Yona
is the Aramaic form of Jonah. When we reopened the church in
Baghdad, the people asked for icons of both Jonah and Thomas –
Mar Thoma.

When I started studying the book of Jonah, it became obvious
to me what a difficult task this prophet had. He had been asked to
share the divine message of the God of Abraham, Isaac and Jacob
regarding repentance and forgiveness with one of the most godless
groups to be found in Scripture. The Assyrians (or Ninevites) contributed largely to the oppression and destruction of the people of
Israel after exiling them from their land.

The Assyrian kingdom stretched from Kirkuk at its southern
point to Amida in the north, through to Edessa in the east on the
border with Persia. The Assyrians were therefore indigenous to
northern Iraq and had as their capital the province of Nineveh.
Their language was Akkadian, still used today by the ancient
Assyrian Church of the East.

Nineveh existed at least 25 centuries before the time of Christ.
It was not an independent state at the time of Jonah but was ruled
by the Sumerians. Assyria had three periods of empire, during

which it conquered Babylonia. The major biblical story connected to the Babylonian conquest is the imprisonment of the young Jewish exiles, Shadrach, Meshach, Abednego and Daniel. Thus one can see why Jonah was negative about being sent to take the Lord's message to such a corrupt and godless people. The amazing thing in the light of this history is that we see how Jonah reluctantly ended up in Nineveh and preached the gospel to this decadent, rebellious people. God devised a means for Jonah, his 'dove', to come and be the channel of peace and mercy. Despite Jonah's resistance, God had his way (involving a very large fish), and the prophetic oracle that he delivered to the Assyrians resulted in their mass conversion to the God of Abraham. They did not merely recant and follow God, but became a radical community committed to their faith.

It is widely thought by theologians and historians that Jonah's influence in Nineveh continued. We know that hundreds of years later, when St Thomas came to Nineveh, there was indeed a strong believing community within the Abrahamic tradition, and the seeds that Jonah had planted had produced a great ongoing harvest. When Thomas arrived after the time of Christ, he told the people about the life, death and resurrection of Jesus and the need to follow him. As a result, the very first Christian community in the whole of Mesopotamia (that is, modern-day Iraq) was created in Nineveh. This legacy has continued until this very day, and Christian believers in Iraq are still referred to as 'Assyrians'. This is an amazing story of what God achieved through forcefully rerouting the most reluctant evangelist over the oceans from Tarshish to Nineveh in a less comfortable version of a submarine.

For many Christians, there are various stereotypical and somewhat negative overtones associated with each of these characters, namely 'Thomas the doubter' and 'Jonah the disobedient prophet'. Sometimes these clichés lead to distorted perception, and certain readers never pass beyond them in their thinking. We must reflect on the Scriptures more deeply and consider the wider lives and legacies of these men. For me, Jonah and Thomas are two of the most inspiring biblical preachers of divine truth. It is known that Thomas started his journey from Jerusalem through miles of desert land – Israel, Jordan and Iraq – and from there through Turkey and on to India. Once in India, Thomas established the first church, and this church was within the Assyrian Christian tradition that had begun with Jonah. The message that came to the Assyrians through Jonah was thus eventually turned into a historic tradition through Thomas. Hence we see an incredible relationship between these men, who lived hundreds of years apart. The word of the Lord is an imperishable seed.

We can learn, through the lives of these prophetic evangelists, great eternal truths about the nature of God that are relevant to us today. We see the mercy, goodness and desperation of God to save and redeem. We see the kindness and patience of God, both in his eagerness to protect his word by preserving the prophet and in his eagerness to protect the truth that had been sown in the heart and mind of Thomas. God was not just protecting a man in a fish; he was protecting a divine scroll, a living oracle, a message that is to us now a book of the Bible, as indeed is the story of Thomas.

This reality of the zealousness of God to protect his word is foundational to his very nature. God's desire to show mercy and loving-kindness and to be in covenantal relationship with all of humankind is driven by his nature. It was love that commissioned Jonah, sent him forth, kept him safe, and placed him as a voice in a region of great hatred and darkness. It was love that met Thomas where he was and empowered him to become one of the most faith-filled, spiritually assured and unwavering preachers of truth in the history of humanity.

Yes, Thomas required assurances and confirmations, but do we not all have times when our faith feels far from invincible? Can we be sure that the rest of the Twelve had no doubts or reservations? Before we judge Thomas and define him as the classic 'doubter', we must reflect both on the political life and confusion of the times and on our own human failings. The reality is that Thomas is probably the disciple most closely aligned with us. We should rather admire this man's transparency and his determination to live in certitude and truth. His great declaration, 'My Lord and my

God!' (John 20.28), the first such declaration recorded, shows us the sense of awe that flooded through him as he embraced Truth and called it his own.

Prayer

Lord, we thank you for the faithfulness of Jonah and Thomas in fulfilling your great commission through their lives and in being mouthpieces of your mercy and your salvation. We ask that you would continue to raise up and anoint mighty men and women of faith to carry your message to the nations. Amen.

49

More than conquerors

Yet in all these things we are more than conquerors through
Him who loved us.
(Romans 8.37 NKJV)

As a child, the eighth chapter of Romans was as much part of my life
as Noddy, or Enid Blyton's Famous Five children's books. My father
would regularly read the commentaries of Dr Martyn Lloyd-Jones on
Romans, and when it came to the eighth chapter he would explain to
me verse by verse what it really meant. I grew up with an understanding that love could not be conquered and that those who loved Father,
Son and Spirit were by nature 'conquerors'. I grew up feeling strong
and assured by this simple yet profound truth which, at that point in
my life, I did not realize would be a truth that I would live out in its
rawest state. When my father died his books were passed to me, and
I was fascinated to see immaculate, almost microscopic, notes in his
commentary on being more than conquerors: 'Yet in all things we are
more than conquerors through Him who loved us.'

In order to fully understand and grasp the victory in this truth,
we must read the preceding verses:

Who shall separate us from the love of Christ? Shall tribulation, or distress, or persecution, or famine, or nakedness, or
peril, or sword? As it is written: 'For Your sake we are killed all
day long; we are accounted as sheep for the slaughter.'
(Romans 8.35–36 NKJV)

The apostle Paul makes it clear that there are indeed many tribula-
tions, including those of an extreme and violent nature, that appear

to separate us from the love of Christ, yet Paul's own revelation was that whether on land or at sea, his darkest hours were still not void of the all-consuming presence and power of divine love.

As Jesus himself states: 'Blessed are those who are persecuted for righteousness' sake, for theirs is the kingdom of heaven' (Matthew 5.10 NKJV). For the suffering Church, these are not just words we say in prayers; this is the reality of our daily experience. In my days in Iraq, our people were slaughtered. Every day, somebody from our community was killed. I counted the numbers daily until the tally exceeded 1,200 and then it became too difficult to count any more. Christians were burned alive in cages, tortured, shot and beheaded. Our people truly were the persecuted; many of their families were murdered.

The promise given by Jesus that the persecuted would be blessed, for 'theirs would be the kingdom', became a living reality for my people. They understood that their call was to be more than conquerors, and that they were both owners and enforcers of an invisible kingdom belonging to an invisible king. This powerful promise that 'theirs is the kingdom' became 'ours is the kingdom'. It was a promise that was received and collectively absorbed. This promise, along with Paul's assurance regarding the unconquerable nature of divine love, and the trust that they could not be separated from the deep affection of their Father and king, gave them strength during times of unspeakable horror and despair.

Paul asks, 'Who shall separate us from the love of Christ?' The answer is not a simple 'No one', but a profound realization that despite the diverse opposition surrounding us on every side, God's love still encircles and sustains us.

God tells his people time and time again not to be afraid as he will fight their battles for them. In Exodus 14.14 (NKJV) we read, 'The LORD will fight for you, and you shall hold your peace.' In Jeremiah 1.19 we read, '"They will fight against you but will not overcome you, for I am with you and will rescue you," declares the LORD.' In other words, the battle is real, but never are we alone.

To be a conqueror is all about love. At the heart of my ministry lie the three words with which I started every service in Iraq: 'Al-hub, *al-hub* and *al-hub'*. We love, love and love. The enemies of love are powerless. They may seek to bring destruction, but they are against the source of all power, which is love. They may cause devastation in this life, but they cannot touch our eternity. Whatever the terror, opposition and persecution, from an eternal perspective those who do not know love are powerless.

In Revelation 12.11, John states that the people of God overcame the evil one 'by the blood of the Lamb and by the word of their testimony'. It is the resurrection blood of the risen Christ that is the very substance of conquest. Likewise, the testimony of his faithfulness throughout the ages, his assured presence, his promises and his worth are great weapons in our hands. Even if we do not see help, rescue, preservation and peace in the way we would wish to see them – through divine intervention; even when the miracles that we need to happen only happen at certain times, the word of our testimony is anchored first and foremost in the Lord's nature rather than his acts. When we understand that he is good and merciful, faithful and true, the word of our testimony becomes all about who he is rather than what he does or does not do. The certitude of the all-powerful blood of Jesus and our confidence in his nature thus work together as a double-edged sword.

Two recent words and visions that my team and I received, both relating to conquest, were the 'banqueting table' and the 'outstretched arm of the Lord'. They both relate to a place of victory through divine providence, and they are both great images within the Psalms.

Psalm 23.5 states: 'You prepare a table [a feast/banquet] before me in the presence of my enemies.' During a time when I was struggling to manage the crises at home and abroad, all I could see was a vision of the banqueting table.

To grasp the significance of this promise from Psalm 23, we need to be aware of the ancient Hebrew tradition of feasting and celebrating. When rich people held a banquet, they would invite only those they felt were important and worthy to attend. So when we are invited to God's banqueting table, we understand how God sees us.

Furthermore, the banquets and feasts were always held outside so that people could see who was invited to the party. These celebrations were not calm, hidden events, but ostentatious and public. If the king held a banquet, those whose names were on the guest list were considered to be the objects of special favour and affection, and they would be served the best food and wine in the land. To be seen at the king's banquet was to make a public statement regarding identity and social worth. Others would look on in envy: they were not invited.

David's understanding of the warrior God who fights through him and for him was one in which conquest, love, provision, favour and joy are all intricately woven together and not hidden from the sight of the enemy. During the darkest times in Baghdad, the reality of the banqueting table was very often within our midst, and recently I have been reminded of its centrality to every battle that we face, particularly to the increasing challenges of providing for a displaced and marginalized community.

The second word that we have had is the 'outstretched arm of the Lord'. In Scripture this phrase is often associated with God's great name and his mighty hand. The outstretched arm is about so many realities: his justice, his provision, his signs and wonders, and most of all his love: 'with a mighty hand and outstretched arm; *His love endures for ever*' (Psalm 136.12). I love this verse because in it I see everything come together. The arm that reaches out in love and grace is the same arm that places the feast before us. Despite the troubles and challenges we may face, this outstretched arm of love is not too short. There is no place it cannot reach.

Prayer

Heavenly Father, we thank you that you have called us to be more than conquerors and that your kingdom is everlasting. We thank you that we have the blood of Jesus and the great testimony of who you are. We thank you for the power of your great love that sustains us in every situation. Amen.

50
Prayer, worship and consecration

Praise be to the name of God for ever and ever;
wisdom and power are his.
He changes times and seasons;
he deposes kings and raises up others.
He gives wisdom to the wise
and knowledge to the discerning.
He reveals deep and hidden things;
he knows what lies in darkness,
and light dwells with him.
(Daniel 2.20–22)

One of my favourite biblical characters is Daniel.

The book of Daniel is an amazing story of the second exodus of the people of Israel, not from Egypt but Babylon. The King of Persia is now in control of Babylonia. The Hebrew people are in exile again, and King Nebuchadnezzar is trying to establish for himself a noble kingdom.

Nebuchadnezzar asked his eunuchs to appoint to the king's court four young leaders from among the Jewish nobility, men of great calibre. Four of the most handsome men were selected and commissioned. Those chosen were Daniel, Hananiah, Mishael and Azariah. The king questioned them all intensively and found that they were far more wise, intelligent and insightful than even the most able members of his own staff. The four were moved into the king's court, and it was decided that they would consume the best food and be given everything they needed to survive well.

They all decided that while they would live in the royal court, they would not consume the royal delights that were bestowed on them. Their first calling was to serve the one God and king of heaven and not the king of Babylon. They therefore decided that under no circumstances would they defile themselves with the food of earthly kings which had been laid before idols: 'But Daniel resolved in his heart that he would not defile himself with the king's food or wine' (Daniel 1.8 BSB).

This act of setting oneself apart and living a life of holy consecration is a model for all of us in every generation. Our decisions should not simply be based on intellectual aspirations and mental striving for self-improvement. Rather we should be like Daniel and resolve deep within our heart that our posture before God is going to be one of unwavering, uncompromised devotion. For me, Daniel's greatest strength was not his exceptional intelligence nor his many abilities, but his resolute heart.

The courtiers were horrified to see these young Jewish nobles living simply on vegetables and water, as they were afraid they would start to look weak and undernourished. Yet the fact was they grew stronger and looked fitter than ever – healthier and better nourished than the other young men of the court. Their diet was not merely vegetables: it was an invisible diet of consuming God's word and feeding on divine presence and revelation.

The king had more than expectations of grandeur. He thought he was a god-like figure who should indeed be worshipped. Nebuchadnezzar created a grand golden idol which was placed in an area of Babylon called Dura. I became very familiar with this location during my years in Baghdad, and in fact it was where many members of my congregation lived before they had to flee to Jordan. I have also spent time at the site where, according to historians, the famous lions' den was likely to have been located, a place that has been revered throughout the centuries.

As the story recounts, the king demanded that three times a day when the trumpets sounded, everybody was to turn towards the king's idol and worship it. For those who refused, the sentence was death in a flaming furnace. Yet Daniel and his friends, Shadrach,

Meshach and Abednego (to use the names the king assigned them), refused to worship the idol and prayed to God three times a day, standing at their window with their faces turned towards Jerusalem. Our eyes should be focused in the right direction, set on things above and not on the things of this world. When our mind and gaze are fixed upon the power, majesty and holiness of the Almighty, we find a place of strength and our faith becomes bolder.

When faced with the terrifying prospect of the fiery furnace, it was this faith that came from the place of unwavering resolve and enabled the men to boldly declare that:

> If the God whom we serve exists, then He is able to deliver us from the burning fiery furnace and from your hand, O king. But even if He does not, let it be known to you, O king, that we will not serve your gods or worship the golden statue you have set up.
> (Daniel 3.17–18 BSB)

This level of faith is rarely seen today, but it was indeed seen among so many of my people in Iraq, including children, as they faced indescribable persecution and martyrdom. Such was their faith in the unseen kingdom that they, like Shadrach, Meshach and Abednego, were able to say, 'Even if God does not save us, we will not turn our faces to another god.' Many as a result were burned alive in the same way that these men were prepared to be. Daniel and his companions grasped the fact that the decree of the earthly king was not final: there was a higher decree and a more powerful king. I had taught my people that there was a higher decree and an invisible kingdom of which they were a part. Believing this was our only hope, our only way to survive, just as it was for Daniel. Even though so many lost their lives, I know they are with the King; they are in eternal glory with 'the God of Daniel'.

Having saved Daniel from the flames, God kept him safe in a den of lions, ensuring that the wild animals could not attack or consume him. God then ensured that even the evil king himself had to publicly turn his face from that which was defiled and false.

Though we live in dark times, we will finally see that every knee shall be forced to bow to the great name that is high above any other name:

> I issue a decree that in every part of my kingdom people must fear and reverence the God of Daniel. 'For he is the living God and he endures for ever; his kingdom will not be destroyed, his dominion will never end.'
> (Daniel 6.26)

Indeed, our God is living, and he promises that those like Daniel, whose faces are turned towards him, will not be covered in shame. Honour, peace and joy eternal will be experienced by those who know and worship him.

Prayer

We thank you, Father, for your faithfulness and mercy throughout the generations, and we thank you for your great and mighty signs and wonders. Help us to have a resolute and unwavering heart like Daniel and his friends as we consecrate ourselves daily to you. Amen.

51
Hanukkah and Christmas

When he had called together all the people's chief priests and
teachers of the law, he asked them where the Messiah was to be
born. 'In Bethlehem in Judea,' they replied, 'for this is what the
prophet has written: "But you, Bethlehem, in the land of Judah,
are by no means least among the rulers of Judah; for out of you
will come a ruler who will shepherd my people Israel."'
(Matthew 2.4-6)

Bethlehem is at the centre of the Christmas story. For me, it is
at the very centre of my life and ministry. My own international
reconciliation ministry came to the fore during the major siege of
the Church of the Nativity in 2002, but I would say that my links
with Bethlehem today are stronger than ever.

The main focus of my life and work there today is Mar Ephrem,
the Syrian Orthodox school which we helped build. Then there is the
Evangelical church where I am officially one of the elders, alongside
pastors Steven and Naim Khoury. One of the programmes we are
working on together is the 'Isaac and Ishmael' project, providing
relief and support for both Jews and Arabs alike. It was an issue of
great joy and surprise when Pastor Steve Khoury actually took relief
to Israeli Jews who had come under attack from Gaza in the south
of Israel. What a wonderful testimony of another blessing out of
Bethlehem!

The nearest Jewish month to December is Kislev, and a lot of
important things have happened in that month. These include two
attacks on the Jerusalem Temple. On 25 Kislev 167 BC, the Syrian
Greeks desecrated the Temple, even sacrificing pigs on the altar.
It was also on 25 Kislev, in the year 164 BC, that the Miracle of

Hanukkah happened. This was when God caused one day's worth of oil to last for eight days. Thus the symbol of Hanukkah is a menorah with eight arms, not seven, remembering this great day and event.

The story of Hanukkah is long and complex, and concerns a small clan of Jewish fighters known as the Maccabees. Their goal was to set Israel free from the Syrian Greeks who had occupied the land under the leadership of Antiochus IV Epiphanes and then tried to impose their own Hellenistic culture. The Temple had been radically defiled. The band of the Maccabees was led by five sons of the temple priest Matthias. The leading son was the famous Judah Maccabee, who to this day is remembered as the hero of Hanukkah. The Feast of Hanukkah is the one Jewish festival not mentioned in the Hebrew Scriptures. Yet it has become a very important feast because it tells us that God always wins in the end and that his victory cannot be undone.

For me in my work, this message of Hanukkah is very important. It says that whoever may try to destroy Israel, they will not succeed. Sadly, in recent years there has been an increase in support for a movement known as Boycott, Divestment and Sanctions (BDS): basically a widespread campaign to discredit Israel, combined with the radical promotion of a Palestinian liberation theology.

The result is that a major part of my work now is trying to resist this growing trend. I am working on the issue closely with the department for religious affairs at the Israeli Ministry of Foreign Affairs. One of the major things I am presently doing is setting up major visits of British and American clergy who either are, or are likely to become, part of the BDS movement. Our aim is to show them the reality and wonder of Israeli and Palestinian society which underlines our whole position of loving both Jews and Palestinians.

For me, this is a further example of what the passage from Matthew chapter 2 is talking about: 'But you, Bethlehem, in the land of Judah, are by no means least among the rulers of Judah; for out of you will come a ruler who will shepherd my people Israel.' The Christ child of Bethlehem is indeed my Lord and Master, but he is also the one who is urging me to show Israel as it really is today. In dealing with this issue, I can't help but think of the similarity to the situation at the first Hanukkah and the attempt to place Hellenistic culture in the Temple.

For me, this whole venture is part of the message of Bethlehem for now. Here once again, Hanukkah and Christmas really do come together in my mission and calling.

Prayer

Lord God, our Saviour, our Lord, we thank you that your message from Bethlehem never ceases to resound and give us purpose and calling. We thank you that the message of Hanukkah speaks to us of the overflowing oil. Amen.

52

Eden restored

COME, LORD JESUS, COME

The LORD will guide you always; he will satisfy your needs
in a sun-scorched land and will strengthen your frame. You
will be like a well-watered garden, like a spring whose waters
never fail.
(Isaiah 58.11)

As I arrive at the final chapter of my journey through the year,
my mind dwells on the promise of 'Eden restored' and my heart
longs for the coming of the Lord. Many of the meditations in this
book have come from Iraq. Genesis 2 says that Eden lay between
the Euphrates and Tigris, so it must have been in Mesopotamia,
which today is Iraq, the land that I love and that has been the centre
of my ministry. I have spent time in the region where Eden is said
to have been located, and the overwhelming feature is the abundance of date palms. The land there is still rich and fertile, and the
seemingly infinite numbers of flourishing trees speak of life and
plenitude.

Eden means 'delight', for it was indeed the delight and hope of
the Lord to create an outpost of heaven on earth, a place of perfect
communion with all that he had created and a place from which his
glory could expand. The physical reality of Eden and my proximity
to it was a constant reminder of the glorious beginnings of creation
and the divine intention for complete restoration.

Another garden that was special to me in Baghdad was the only
public park in the city. It was situated near the rivers, and here on
Friday nights we would take the young people and enjoy church

picnics. God would often speak to me as I walked through this place. There is something special about gardens: they are places of tranquillity, family community and spiritual intimacy.

The more I contemplate gardens, the more I consider how the entire Bible is centred on three key gardens and leads us on a journey from the first to the third – which itself is all about the restoration of the first. Today we pass from Eden to Gethsemane, and we end in the garden of the Lord within the great eternal city as described in the book of Revelation, a place of great flourishing and fruitfulness that was seen in a vision by both Ezekiel and the apostle John.

Gethsemane is a place I often visit during my times in Jerusalem. As I pause among those ancient olive trees – some of which, according to historians, geologists and professors of botany, may well date back two thousand years – I, along with many others, find it to be a place of great contemplation. Sitting there, I feel a sense of intense suffering – I feel as if I enter something that I have not yet touched in terms of human anguish and emotional agony. I am awed as I consider how 'everything' came from this place of 'nothing'. I look across over the city of Jerusalem, and my mind ponders the resurrection, the first appearances of the risen Messiah, the Ascension, and that glorious Shavuot when the Holy Spirit was poured out among Jews from so many nations.

As with Eden, which means 'delight', the meaning of Gethsemane is relevant. It means 'olive press', and oh, how true it is, both for Jesus and for us, that from the place of great crushing, fresh oil is released, and an unquenchable flow of anointing is produced. Without the crushing, there is no fragrance, there is no oil. The agony that Jesus went through in that garden related to the most brutal form of physical, spiritual and emotional crushing that any human could suffer, and yet, from this crushing and pressing, the oil of Shavuot, the anointing of the Spirit, was released to all nations. In the place of pain, great joy was released. That which was lost and forfeited in the first garden was starting to be restored in the second, as the second Adam prepared to offer himself as the one eternal sacrifice.

This book has described aspects of the agony and ecstasy of a life and ministry in some of the most difficult and dangerous places in the world, and these continue to be part of my calling. Yet we all know that the place of crushing can be anywhere – in our own homes, in our places of work. One does not need to be in the Middle Eastern war zone to identify with these stories: we all experience our own agony and ecstasy, and we all need to respond, 'Come, Lord Jesus.'

As we come to the final garden as described in Revelation, we move from Gethsemane (Eden 'being' restored) to Eden Restored:

> Then the angel showed me a river of the water of life, as clear as crystal, flowing from the throne of God and of the Lamb down the middle of the main street of the city. On either side of the river stood a tree of life, bearing twelve kinds of fruit and yielding a fresh crop for each month. And the leaves of the tree are for the healing of the nations.
> (Revelation 22.1-2 BSB)

This is a scene that fills me with deep joy, hope, faith and anticipation, for as heaven comes to earth and God's plan for divine restoration unfolds, we will see abundant life and a full reversal of all that does not belong in this garden. Pain will be removed and tears wiped away, whole nations will be healed, sorrow will turn into joy, poverty will be replaced by abundance, and barren places will become full of life. The land will be cleansed from the sin that entered Eden, and access to the Tree of Life that was once made inaccessible will be restored to the redeemed. The healing oil released from the place of crushing in Gethsemane will flow like rivers:

> The threshing floors will be full of grain, and the vats will overflow with new wine and olive oil. I will repay you for the years that the swarming locust ate, the young locust, the destroying locust, and the devouring locust – My great army that I sent against you.
> (Joel 2.24-25 HCSB)

I believe that many of these realties can already be experienced because of the redemptive work of Christ, and it is my prayer that we will see the earth filled with his glory and he will return to us soon:

> Then he told me, 'Do not seal up the words of the prophecy of this scroll, because the time is near. Let the one who does wrong continue to do wrong; let the vile person continue to be vile; let the one who does right continue to do right; and let the holy person continue to be holy.'
>
> 'Look, I am coming soon! My reward is with me, and I will give to each person according to what they have done.' (Revelation 22.10–12)

As I contemplate these verses once again, I smile to myself because I hear the voices of all my young children and teenagers in Baghdad resounding in my ears. Whenever I quoted this scripture they would say, 'But Daddy, why is soon such a long time in coming? He said he was coming back soon and that was two thousand years ago!' I would always explain to them that heaven's timing is very different from our timing. As with every generation, we expect, we pray, we wait, and we hope that it will be soon . . . and very soon.

Prayer

Father, we ask you to plant your garden in our souls. In our daily service please bless us, strengthen us, keep us close to you, and help us know you and be known by you, so that our thoughts and deeds will please you for evermore. Amen.

About Jerusalem MERIT

Jerusalem MERIT was founded in 2018 in order to support the Iraqi refugee community in Jordan. MERIT stands for Middle East Reconciliation International.

The ambassador of Jerusalem MERIT, the Revd Canon Dr Andrew White, formerly known as the 'Vicar of Baghdad', is a major pioneer and religious leader in the Middle East, supporting Iraqi Christians, Jews and Muslims, and engaging in conflict resolution during the many years of national political and religious conflict and turmoil in the region.

Jerusalem MERIT supports the Iraqi refugee community, now largely residing in Jordan. Jerusalem MERIT's projects include the provision of comprehensive education and medical assistance through the establishment of a school and medical clinic, and the provision of food-stamp programmes and housing assistance for Iraqi refugees of all faiths.

Jerusalem MERIT also supports Canon Andrew White in his international reconciliation and diplomatic work, focusing principally on the Middle East.

For further information, to subscribe to our newsletter and to make donations, please contact:

1 Rookery House
Grove Farm
Crookham Village
Fleet GU51 5RX
UK

Email: hello@jerusalemmerit.org
Tel.: +44 (0) 1428 723939
(Jordan) +962 791749303
(Israel) +972 546365126

Bible acknowledgements

The quotation marked RSV is taken from the Revised Standard Version of the Bible, copyright © 1946, 1952 and 1971 by the Division of Christian Education of the National Council of the Churches of Christ in the USA. Used by permission. All rights reserved.